Ebb and Flow

or
The Rhythm in the World
of the Spirit

Johann Baptist Krebs

Ebb and Flow

or
The Rhythm in the World
of the Spirit

Where wisdom speaks, there you are safe;
Where cleverness reigns, you ensnare yourself.
Hence hear the voice of wisdom everybody,
Wherever you are, then you'll work for good and right.

Johann Baptist Krebs

translated by Kerry A Nitz

K A Nitz
WHANGANUI, NEW ZEALAND

Ebbe und Flut, oder Der Rhythmus in der Geisterwelt
2nd edition published in German 1915
under the pseudonym J. Kernning

This translation into New Zealand English
Copyright © K A Nitz 2025
All rights reserved

ISBN: 978-0-473-73412-1

Table of Contents

Translator's Note 7
Introduction 9
Conservatism 13
Progress 19
Principles of Progress 23
The Association Members 27
The Flight 31
The Conversion 35
Ebb and Flow 41
Self-Reflection 51
The Passport 57
America 67
A New Star 71
The Development Periods 77
Stability of the Laws 83
The Best State Institution 89
Ebb and Flow 95
Home 99
Diversity in Unity 101

Translator's Note

For the English translation of Bible texts I have made use of the King James Version. Where I thought it would be helpful I have also inserted missing Biblical citations in the footnotes.

The occasionally somewhat idiosyncratic approach of the author to presenting dialogue has also been retained in part.

***

Introduction

Ebb and flow must alternate constantly because standstill would be at once death. Going forwards and backwards is a law of nature. Anyone who merely wanted to breathe in would explode, but anyone who endeavoured only to breathe out would have to wither. Forwards and backwards, breathing in and out, ebb and flow are conditions under which alone activity, life and maturity are possible.

In the forties of the nineteenth century we saw Europe in a commotion where you did not know when the flame of outrage would spread over all its lands and turn everything upside down. Not only amongst the uneducated and oppressed, no, even amongst the most esteemed families, with men and youth who possessed the most distinguished reputations for morality, lawfulness, and every social virtue, the spirit of outrage had taken root, and phenomena became visible which you did not know how to explain. No state administration, and even if yet so good, no regal virtue, and even if yet so gleaming, gave guarantees for the calm of a land, and it was no different than if a spirit of hell were strolling amongst humanity in order to forge ever new plans and fanaticise the participants.

At that time the naturalist Braun, Doctor of Philosophy, lived with one of his friends, the estate owner Steinwart in G., who had sent his son Gustav to the university in order to continue and complete his studies. Braun, who knew the character of his time better than his friend, expressed great reservations with the departure of Gustav to his destination. The father, full of confidence in the principles and probity of his son, placated his friend and said, "If my son were ever able to deviate from the path of lawfulness, I would not recognise him as my son anymore, and my heart would have to break over it." Even the mother, who was present, spoke for Gustav in that she considered it impossible that he would ever abandon the path of duty and give his parents sorrow. Braun indeed responded that the discontented appeared not with the banner of lawlessness and of injustice, but rather as defenders of truth and savers of humanity and there a young disposition could easily be seduced and led astray from the path of duty. Gustav gave the most sacred assurances; father and mother relied on his promise and Braun finally said, "Heaven guide it." There he was referring to the University of G. Also Braun, who had already long since received an invitation to V. in order to make a few arrangements there in respect to natural history, likewise went off on the journey and thus father and mother were left behind quite alone and could only slowly accustom themselves to the stillness which had entered the house.

The first year passed for Gustav without temptation. He did not exclude himself from the student societies, but did so without letting himself getting carried away by their activities. Since he was efficiently prepared for university and also now always diligent, the professors granted him undivided praise, and when he came home at the first holidays, his parents, particularly his mother, did not know how they could make him happy enough. This love and care naturally reinforced the bond between parents and son still more, and he vowed to them and to himself to never do anything which could disturb their happiness.

He returned to the university at the end of the holidays with new resolve for good behaviour and diligence, and lived several months almost entirely for himself. But at once decent fellows who stood in good repute approached him and heaped him with favours and attestations of friendship. He ascribed this to the likeness of ages and the love for the sciences, and abandoned himself to the impressions of their courtesy all the more when he heard of nothing in their company but enlightenment, virtue, and the welfare of humanity. He wrote to his father about the new acquaintances without raising his

Introduction

suspicions in the slightest. If Braun had been present, he would probably have looked more deeply into it and have advised the father to remove his son as quickly as possible from his current residence. Only he was not a guardian spirit who would have warned and drawn the inexperienced boy out of the labyrinth. The snare was laid and we will soon see the victim so entangled that he would have been lost without the help of a friend.

***

Conservatism

In the house next to him there lived an academic who had already graduated and had only remained back at the university to study thoroughly the history of Germany and to this end still used the library and the advice of the professors. His behaviour was extremely ordered. Logical in his talk and actions, in his way of life and his studies, he distinguished himself by old German garb, old German customs, and by a full beard. Up to then Gustav had neither paid any attention to him, nor had he to Gustav. Now they got to know each other as neighbours and each seemed to find pleasure in the other. Gustav admired the deep knowledge and the moral steadfastness of his new acquaintance, but the latter admired the sense of righteousness and the persistent industry of the former. Both met up from this time on frequently and discussed the state of culture, jurisprudence, and all the affairs of the peoples. Gustav felt so drawn to his new friend that he made a report about it to his father and praised the stroke of fate which had given him such a guide. His father rejoiced in this friendship and asked his son to not let such an opportunity to go past unused, because you often drew on private paths more thorough knowledge than in the mechanical ways of the school lecture. Gustav was delighted over such remarks and abandoned himself to the leadership of his friend unconditionally.

When they were together one evening, the conversation turned to natural law, the study of which Gustav was looking forward to already in advance. Brandheim, that being the name of his friend, responded with, "There is no natural law anymore, because we are too far removed from nature. Had we only a national law once again, then we would want to leave natural law to the philanthropists. But even the nations have no right anymore. Everything has gone under through arbitrary presumptions, through weakness and feudalism. There are rights, but no right. We have laws, but not from the character of the people, instead borrowed from Greeks, Latinists, and Frenchmen. What should pandects be to us? How could Justinian-like institutions be fit for Germany? Would the Napoleonic Code be of use to us? Certainly not. The most essential thing which must happen in Germany is to make one Germany again. We do not have any Germany now, but rather German lands. We have no German law, but rather feudal and great lord laws. In every land it is different, in every earldom, almost on every knight's seat we encounter arrangements which have no trace of Germanness, and we, we legal scholars, are called to put our knowledge into practice in this Babylon in order to bring or prepare Babylonian actions, setting aside where it is not prosecuted."

Gustav had listened approvingly and asked whether in Germany national institutions and laws had ever existed. Brandheim replied, "Three points of light are delivered by German history where we see pure nationality. The first is before the invasion of the Romans into Gaul, where they still found themselves in the pure, one would like to say, in the mythological primal state. The second we see at the time of Arminius, where German character opposed the German colossus and set the land free. The third begins with Charlemagne and shines through several centuries under the sceptre of German kings and emperors, where all the greats stood under a freely elected head and obeyed him in war and peace. This was the midday sun of Germany. Through unity it was politically great, through the statelessness of the emperor free, and through inborn probity, and strength of soul and body superior to all other peoples, it had achieved a peak so that no realm of the world and of history could compare itself with it. Our time aims at this last state — from the multiplicity to make a great unity is the idea of all true and great thinkers and patriots, and whoever can contribute just a small bit to this great transformation must as human, as citizen and son of a glorious fatherland dedicate themselves to this plan and seize every means to carry it out."

"What can the individual do here?", asked Gustav full of expectation. Brandheim responded, "The single bee cannot fill the beehive with honey and wax, but where thousands are active, the work becomes easy."

"But where", asked Gustav further, "should the thousands come from?" Brandheim replied, "Instinct guides the bees to assemble. Instinct, the love of the fatherland, must lead the genuine German to live and to work for his fatherland. It is only about awakening the idea, spreading it, and animating it ever anew, then in the end will come what must come, and Germany's happiness and political greatness will be reproduced without you knowing how it came about."

For Gustav the idea of spreading such ideas had the most interest. It is a peculiarity of the age of youth to constantly find new ways to be of use to humanity and to work for it. Here a path was opened for him, and hence he grasped the matter with all the warmth of his youthful, uncorrupted heart. He said, "What you have said is of great importance, and if I can serve the fatherland, then I will exert all my powers to making myself capable of it. But is surely the benefit which you expect from your plan also certain? Are you convinced that a unity is to be produced and from this the hoped-for fruits will come?"

Brandheim responded, "What I am saying is not the fruit of a stirred up imagination, but rather of the serious inquiry into the history of our fatherland. When was Germany great? Under Charlemagne, under the Saxon Ottos, under Frederick Barbarossa, Henry the Fowler, and a gleaming row of Hohenstaufens. An emperor without possessing land, free of all private interests, ruled the entire land; all the princes and dukes were subject to him and had to sacrifice their private considerations to the whole. He, the emperor, stood above all and had eyes only for the welfare and the strength of that entrusted to him. Everything emanated from one, all gathered around one. He was elected publicly, his judgements were public, he stood a German man amongst Germans and brothers and could not rule in any other way than in the national spirit. — Indeed it is said those old forms have become outdated and would not be suitable for our time anymore. — Unfortunately their introduction would run into resistance, but not on account of their unsuitability, rather on account of the corruption of the German character which has lost its stamp through Gallomania, which at most has been preserved in the middle class and domestic relationships. But give back to our glorious German nation what it possessed in former times in its greatness, and it will quickly recognise its sanctum and raise itself to power and independence. Stability is the soul of law-giving. Stable are the laws of nature — for the course of the stars is unchangeable. May a winter also be colder, a summer drier than the next, that does not change the character of the earth. Likewise the nationalities — they remain under all circumstances the same, whatever storms darken the political skies. Hence away with the constant striding forward, with the reformations in the area of civil and criminal law-giving. Nature is our teacher, and the same conservatism which reigns in her must also find itself with nations, otherwise the peoples are a plaything of chance, of ambition, of the chasing of ideas where each would like to see his bit of thought admired in a new institution."

Gustav felt the excellence of these views, only he thought you should under these circumstances not worry any longer about intimacy and rules of procedure, but rather set forth to the government and peoples openly and systematically what was necessary so that the wished-for state could be prepared properly and put into practice. Brandheim asserted that everything will happen, only you must go to work with caution in order to not close the door on the great plan straightaway at the start. Gustav saw this, but asserted that you would be permitted to count on him under all circumstances. Brandheim took pleasure in this assurance, and left with the words that there was no higher calling for a German than to dedicate yourself to the fatherland.

Gustav, when he was alone, thought over what he had heard and in order to give a proper account of it, he sat down at his writing desk and sought to put it down on paper as systematically as possible. He worked almost the entire night through and when he had slept for a few hours towards morning, he got down to the study of law with doubled zeal in order to become competent to separate the true German from others and to be able to shine a guiding light through words and text for his countrymen.

***

Progress

In this year nothing else new happened for Gustav. Brandheim remained his friend and teacher, almost in all subjects of knowledge, and he worked himself so assuredly out of the usual dust of the school that he was often described by Brandheim with the name of a philosopher of nature who carried everything within himself and needed merely to bring it to light. He accustomed himself through Brandheim's contact to a sharpness of thinking that his teachers were astonished over, and distinguished him at every opportunity.

Conservatism was his basic law. Legality, founded on nationality, seemed to him a necessity of nature, and when he came into contact with alternatively-minded men, with men of progress, with propagandists, it became quite eerie for him, because these men too called upon necessity, upon laws of nature and substantiated it with convincing reasons. Stability, they said, draws rottenness to itself. Pour the purest water into a container and let it rest there, then it ferments, becomes impure, and is hardly still usable for the wetting of manure. What have China and other empires obtained through conservatism? Nothing. They stand there sunken impotently within themselves and are never sure when progress will mess them up.

Such utterances made him indeed not untrue to his views, but he felt unsettled because he could not properly contradict them. He spoke with Brandheim about them, and the latter said, "The world divides itself into two views, in that of conservatism and that of progress. Each party has reasons for their view, and I advise everybody to examine the matter exactly before they conclude for one of them. I pay homage to conservatism and would sacrifice everything to it, especially in our fatherland, and if need must, my life. What the propagandists say about China and other empires has no basis, in that precisely China has flourished under law for eight thousand years, meanwhile Greece and Rome were ruined because of sheer improvements and laws in less than a thousand years. Every thing has its maturity — as soon as this has occurred, the growth stops and the fruits appear. If the trees grew for evermore, what would we get from them? They would finally by virtue of their height and extent outweigh their roots and collapse — of fruits there could not be any talk at all anymore. Thus human society with mature laws, tested by experience and fitting to the character of the people. The child inherits such from the parents, grows up within them, and makes them his own as if they were interwoven into his nature, so that for him not following them would be more difficult than the most punctual exercise of them. Hence away with the propaganda*. Death to them and downfall, whether they emanate from thrones or rebels. Curse every vacillator who does not have strength enough to stay on a firm standpoint, wanting to always be reflected in new phenomena and be delighted by change at the cost of the true happiness of the people. I say and emphasise, if it must be, with my blood: the world will not ever have peace until it renounces its addiction to constantly new laws, and throws itself into the arms of the true, the solid, in one word, conservatism."

Gustav felt quite thrilled by such views and could not grasp why the authorities themselves made so many sacrifices to progress. He made his plan and gave himself his word to work for conservatism with all his powers, and so as not to be idle, he began with himself, gave himself rules to live by, lived by them with the greatest punctuality and obtained thereby a strength of character which raised him far above his years and obtained general respect for him. You can easily think that all the association members and student fraternities which were forming everywhere at that time will have

---

* [Tr.: note that in the context of the mid-19th century Germany of the setting, the word "Propaganda" stood for spreading left-wing political ideas.]

directed their eyes at him. But mainly it was the propagandists who would have liked to have had him in their association and hence tried everything to win him over.

Ludwig Frohbart, a countryman of Gustav, who had been at school with him as a boy, found himself though a year later at the university. Both had meanwhile, apart from the usual academic circumstances, not arrived in any close connection. Frohbart was a decided propagandist and saw not only the fortunes of the fatherland, but that of entire humanity in a progress in all the branches of knowing and doing, even if forcibly imposed. He was a leading member of an association which was incorporated and formally constituted to this end. The basic statutes came from his association and were so convincing and guiding that already private men, indeed even civil servants had been led to acknowledge them to be good and to join them. Several members of the intended association reproached Frohbart for not having already long since drawn such a solid fellow as Gustav into the association. Frohbart knew of Gustav's idea of conservatism and repudiated the reproaches being made, but promised to do everything possible to win him over to their aims. We see thus a new danger for Gustav which, even if it is not capable of ensnaring him, does so much as to cause him to surrender a constituted association, conservatism, unconditionally and thereby almost decide his future fate. Since Frohbart is coming into closer contact with Gustav, we also want to hear the confession of beliefs of his association in order to be able to judge finally to what extent the fortunes of the peoples may have been enlisted in them.

***

Principles of Progress

Frohbart sought, in accordance with his promise, to enter into a more familiar relationship with Gustav. Academic acquaintances were quickly made and since the natural association of being from the same region already connected them, you saw them from now on, sometimes at home, sometimes on walks, frequently together. For a long time Frohbart was unable to succeed in speaking calmly over political views, since Gustav, whenever Frohbart came too close to his conservatism, became passionate and threatened to end the amicable relationship. Frohbart meanwhile maintained so much calm that he succeeded each time in avoiding the break and bringing about a mood which made it possible to speak about the present topic. Gustav one day said, "You want to seduce me, make me give up my views which have grown together with my blood and hence can also change only with the loss of it. But, in order to show you that I am certain of my matter, I will allow you to dig out your ideas from a seemingly gladdening propaganda, but desire that you also listen to my views, and to the extent they do not please you, do not trouble me further and want to force on me principles which have never been consistent with the character of the Germans and never be consistent."

Frohbart replied, "So be it. There is only one political truth, but also only one path which leads to it. So listen then! — In order to show you how fundamentally I and all who are of my mind go to work, I must tell you that our investigations begin with the origin of humanity. The human steps imperfectly, without experience and reflection from the hand of nature, feeling and knowing nothing but that he is hungry, that he is freezing and he is in need of calm and sleep. What else could be expected of such imperfect beings than that they learned from the animals how they nourished themselves, mated, build nests and dens, and thus through the instinct of nature which the human lacks eked out their life. The animals were the first teachers of humans, and only after the latter had achieved the ability of making their own experiences, did the son learn from the father, the grandson from the son, and the great-grandchildren from their parents and forebears. In this manner the human race flew up to the heights where we now see it, and will not stand still until it has reached the highest peak and can say this is my maturity, my culmination.

We see in world history nations rising and falling and are often tempted to believe the culture of humanity moves in a constant circle and is required again and again to descend as soon as it has reached a great height. This falling and rising, however, is only a seeming one, is the clambering up on the scaffolding before a house whose girders are not yet properly fastened. Let us obtain for the erection of our building firstly firm ground, then the noblest friends of humanity, the most skilled workers must be collected in order to secure a refuge for humanity which can never ever be destroyed and in which all can gather.

You will ask what then can we, the individuals, do with such a giant undertaking? — To the uninhibited the answer comes easily, when he considers in what blindness, in what darkness the human still lives. Dead forms have taken the place of a living culture, of a progress of civilisation, of enlightenment, of the laws of association, and obstruct humanity in its natural growth. Understanding or better cleverness reigns much amongst humans, but the mind they must not use. Instead of thinking, they are taught in schools and state affairs to obey and believe. Instead of awakening the reason, you fill the brain with political and religious dogmas which have neither sense nor understanding. The feeling of natural freedom is a crime. Equal rights and duties are barely still material for idylls — in social life they stand under the heading of great crimes. How then can the spirit develop? How does the reason come into action when you shackle and suppress it? The reason alone is the true giver of laws. It alone knows what is good or harmful for the human. Let us support reason in its rights, in which alone gratifying conformity to law lies, then we will need no government, no religion, and no antique customs anymore, which are all only present for drawing the bonds of slavery ever firmer about humanity.

Do not be put off that I have become a bit bitter — only how can a feeling heart calmly bear the horror which still reigns amongst humanity? The poor countryman does not possess any time anymore to think about the truths of life; from early morning to late in the evening he must work in order to nourish himself and his family poorly, but at the same time fill the stores of the rich with the fruits of his industry. The rich possess so much, sacrifice too much time to pleasures and idleness to obtain a few minutes to think about the laws of reason. The light to which the eyes turn is suppressed. With all the efforts which are given to teach and to learn, nothing essential is done and achieved though because everywhere compulsion reigns and thereby not only is the activity of reason hampered, but it is also suppressed and banished from human society.

From this easily arises what the actual friend of humanity, the world citizen has to do; and truly, the work is so enormous that the cleaning of the Augean stables is just child's play in comparison. When we see the rawness and the perverse concepts of many country people! When we turn our eyes to the Orient, what darkness reigns still there! And why? Perhaps from lack of teaching institutions or teachers? No, from lack of freedom to be permitted to investigate and make use of the experiences of history rationally. The human possesses so much cultural ability that, if you let his desire to learn have free play, he learns and comprehends everything and knows how to take care of his own welfare as well as that of others. Therefore give the human free life, free thinking and acting and he will find the secure way to the destiny of his existence."

Gustav offered his hand to his countryman after this talk and said, "I see the welfare of humanity lies as close to your heart as it does to mine. If you strive to achieve this on a different path, then I can only regret that we do not stroll together; but I must give full justice to your zeal and show you my respect. Would it then not be possible to unite our views, and, since we are not capable of producing the welfare of the whole, to limit ourselves to our fatherland which needs no progress, rather a wise, secure form of government which emerges from the character of the people and is written in the heart of every German. What then have those political revolutions which we have seen in history and before our own eyes created for us? Nothing but war and disaster, mistrust and poverty, perversions of the law and confusions in trade. Every state seeks its own advantage, without caring how much the other suffers under it. And what arises from this? Hate and distrust amongst the members of a nation who have the same origin, speak one language, and are born to love each other and to have before their eyes the welfare of others as well as their own. Should we through the fantastic idea of progress surely spread new reformations, new confusions amongst our countrymen? There may God preserve us from it. The single, safest thing which we can do is seize the spirit of the time to distance the ungerman and by and by work ourselves into the spirit of national institutions so that it penetrates the people, shows the princes the necessity to hear the voice of their subjects, and in this way, even if forced, though by appearance still voluntarily, to place ourselves again under the original laws of the fatherland. See, that is my view, my innermost conviction. Consider what I said, and if you can not unite yourself with me, then our hearts shall not not become foreign to each other. The thought that you love the fatherland no less than I do will allow me to always recognise in you a friend who, even if walking on different paths, bears though noble dispositions in his heart.

***

The Association Members

The history of the time shows us here two noble youths who were full of holy zeal to do something for the benefit of the fatherland without considering that the fire of youth is not suited to changing state institutions and putting a stick in the spokes of the wheel of time. The imagination had shackled them and each drew the band which entangled him with like-minded people ever tighter so that they finally saw themselves indissolubly bound by oaths and signatures. The difference of views and plans kept Gustav and Frohbart from this time on at a strange distance, where neither seemed to trust the other and carefully hid his doings. Both parties had formally constituted themselves and were sending missionaries through all the lands and cities. The members for conservatism limited themselves indeed mainly to German. The others, however, knew no country borders; the world was their aim, to raise it to the peak of freedom, of happiness, and of enlightenment was their task, and hence were sworn for the downfall of the asiatic despots as much as the European governments. They saw in every existing institution nothing but hindrances to progress and hence their emissaries agitated in Russia as eagerly as in Germany, France, and Italy. The entire surface of the earth seemed to be their property, to be a region conquered by their ideas, which could not escape them anymore at all. Both parties carried on thus for several years and expanded without having the appearance of being observed, or as if anyone would have the courage of working against them.

Gustav and Frohbart had finished their studies and left the university without, however, being disloyal to the words given to their brothers. Many such members had already entered offices or otherwise chosen a branch of employment. They numbered on their lists of the most distinguished of almost all classes: legal scholars, clergymen, soldiers, doctors, foremen, economists had joined this or that party and awaited only the most favourable moment to appear publicly. Only the matter found the greatest hindrance in itself. With such numbers of members it could not be lacking that the original ideas did not finally step into the background and other plans of revolution had to take their place. Finally a party of exalted heads formed which put up the principle that the world was too corrupt to be improved and made receptive for the highest goal of happiness and of freedom. From the ashes the phoenix of general welfare must rise. Only from rubble can the tree of true freedom sprout and grow. Only from the decay can the salvation of humanity arise, hence it is necessary to prepare a general world revolution and to let it rage as a judgement of God. From these renewers of the world yet another party spun off which had not yet stopped nourishing plans for a political reorganisation and which declared the principle of a perfect equality of possessions to be legally valid. They said the rulers and rich have possessed their unfair estate for too long already and must therefore be called to account. Wealth and power were the greatest crimes and since the happiness of the people next to such can not exist, then it is necessary to judge and exterminate them.

Gustav and Frohbart heard such utterances with horror. Only the current was too powerful, they could not dam it anymore. The only thing which remained for them to do was to keep alive the laws of humanity, which were expressed by the association members themselves as the highest principle, in order to not see all humanity denied.

Up until this point in time the authorities had taken no notice of these intrigues. They were considered to be student excesses which would disintegrate of themselves. Only since the French propaganda was spreading ever further, since the

The Association Members

society for human rights as active branch of it had several times already raised its banner, and traces of those institutions amidst all classes of the people even in Germany were appearing, the authorities were not permitted to remain idle anymore and had to exert everything to call the conspirators to account. Soon they succeeded in uncovering a few locations of their meetings and even obtaining lists of names. Now the first step had been taken, you were not permitted to stand still, and hence several members were immediately put under arrest. Now you became aware for the first time that you had opportunity to test the firmness of character of those arrested, the importance and the methodical nature of the conspiracies. You saw that you were not dealing with student societies, but rather with a constituted association which was extending its arms into all regions and lands. Now it was about getting to know the tendencies, might, and means of assistance of the association members in order to set about them with appropriate pressure. To describe how that was all carried out is not the task of these lines. Each of our contemporaries has seen with their own eyes in what way the young Germany, the young Italy, the propaganda of our neighbouring states were finally put before the court and the proper punishment handed down.

***

The Flight

Around this time Dr Braun returned from his journey, visited Gustav's father and asked after the son's health. After he heard that this young man had completed his studies and begun his career as a lawyer in B., he asked whether Gustav had never been tempted to connect with the so-called demagogues. The father replied, "There my son is much too patriotically minded. Nothing is above the welfare of his German fatherland, and he would place his own body in line if an attack threatened it. Braun, who was quite informed with respect to the entirety of connections, said, "There reigns in our days a twofold sort of love of the fatherland, one legitimate and one illegitimate. I hope that Gustav possesses the first and I would like to know how he tends to express himself over it orally and in writing." The father told of what he knew, showed finally Gustav's letters, and Braun recognised at first glance the danger in which the son of his friend was hovering. He said with great emotion, "Gustav must go far away from the fatherland, otherwise he is lost. He belongs to an association which is not aiming at anything less than the overthrow of all forms of government in his fatherland, and who knows what new ones it will introduce." The father, convinced of the uprightness of his son, did not want to hear of such a suggestion. But the doctor said, "Gustav is nice, that I maintain myself. The love for the fatherland, for humanity, in short, the most sacred urges have moved him to enter into associations which, even if quite pure to begin with, have degenerated into the most criminal plans and are drawing every participant, whether good or bad, into the abyss. Gustav must leave. His honour and his life are at stake. Endure it, father, as well as you can! — Strengthen his mother for a perhaps year-long absence of her son and even if it were lifelong, then it would yet be better for both parents than knowing the son was in jail and trembling night and day for his life. Just get together the means of travel quickly. I will move him to flee and not leave him until I know he is in safety." The father still did not want to hear anything about flight, but when the doctor brought to his attention the daily arrests of respectable young people, he became apprehensive and said, "I cannot believe it, but the concern for my son does not allow me to oppose it any longer." He went to a cupboard, took two tubes of gold, each of fifty ducats, and handed them to the doctor with the words, "Rescue my son if danger threatens him. This gold I was wanting to put in the bank today and for someone other than him. Rescue his honour and his life. He is indeed my greatest wealth. I will make his mother aware when I know he is in safety." The doctor offered his hand to the father, went by post-chaise and travelled, equipped only with the most necessary things, to B. where Gustav was staying.

The latter was pleasantly surprised when he saw the doctor again after so many years. But his surprise reached the highest degree when he learned the cause of the unexpected visit. For a long time he did not want to hear anything of flight, because he consider such a thing to be shameful; but when Braun commanded him to in the name of his parents, he agreed to leave for a few weeks, and to wait on the events in Germany in a border town of France, and in the most favourable moment to be straightaway again at the place of his determination up to then. The doctor liked this suggestion and he urged for the greatest haste, because he would not be safe anymore for another day, perhaps even an hour. Gustav, although he did not consider this danger to be so great, had himself issued a pass for a few weeks, put his papers in order, and was travelling away with the doctor even before it was evening. Along the way the latter made know to his fugitive the measures which the government was being forced to take and brought him to the decision to likewise move to flight his former schoolmate Frohbart, to whose place of residence the

The Flight

road led. "He is", said Gustav, "more involved than I am, for he is a key agent of the progressives to are spread everywhere." The doctor knew the Frohbart family and was pleased to be able to spare them much sorrow through this step. They arrived at H., Frohbart's place of residence, just as morning was breaking. Gustav immediately went to him, woke him from his sleep, made him aware of his flight and called upon him to accompany him. Frohbart, already suspecting nothing good for a few day, immediately agreed, used a pass for France which he had obtained a few days before for some business, and two hours later sat with Gustav and the doctor in the carriage, who doubled the tip everywhere in order to get across the border with his two demagogues safely. They crossed it at Saarlouis, but continued without stopping to Metz where they were determined to stay for the time being and wait out the events in Germany. They arrived there in the evening, entered the Hotel N. N., and joked over the doctor's expressed joy at knowing his two charges were safe.

***

The Conversion

Although the travellers were tired and the doctor suggested dining in the room and going to bed afterwards, the two fugitives wanted nonetheless to go down into the barroom in order to hear the political mood of the guests and perhaps establish an acquaintance with somebody. For the first point they found complete satisfaction, for they heard utterances which they would not have been permitted to make in their closed gatherings. Reckless censure over ministers and king, contempt for all institutions and laws, revolutionary phrases and allusions comprised the content of the conversation. It all breathed of — not freedom — but rather lack of restraint which would rather remove every law without considering that then nobody would be protected anymore and they would also have no means anymore for achieving anything good. Our two demagogues were genuine friends of the people, and penetrated by their favourite ideas, they considered any deviation from them to be sacrilege and an outrage against humanity. Indeed Frohbart recalled that he too had once spoken in this manner, but only in private; here, however, he saw himself in an unpleasant mirror. They finally went to bed and put off until the morning speaking with the doctor about their further plans.

When they had breakfasted the next day and had put their travel things in order a bit, they went to his room in order to ask further advice for the following days. He responded to their inquiry, "You are safe, and that can be enough for us for the time being. What should happen in the future will depend upon the news which we expect from home." The two fugitives still though his fear was exaggerated in that the authorities would not be permitted so easily to dare to resist the spirit of the people and to stand against the powerful current which was close to breaching the banks, if they did not want to summon their own downfall. The doctor responded, "The authorities stand on firm ground. Their reputation and their might are sanctified by time and tradition. When they call, hundreds of thousands follow from devotion to the old ruling house to which they render homage, for which they pray in the family circle, in schools and churches, out of awe for the laws to which they, their parents, and their ancestors swore loyalty. Here one rules a generation planted in flesh and blood, in reason and emotion, which cannot be destroyed by exalted heads and fanatical talk. Lead your gathered together hordes against such a firmly ranged, ordered troop and it will be beaten by the sight of it; not from fear, but rather because the previously hallowed banner of their princely house, which they are now resolved to desecrate, fills them at the same time with reverence and horror. The people themselves will undertake nothing against the government. The members of the association, at the head of a few work-shy craftsmen, are too weak, are dreamers, not united amongst themselves and will entice themselves in the end into the trap. — You, my friends, are in safety, are, if disorder arises, not present and maintain a passivity towards the association members and government which must redound in no case to your disadvantage, but probably to your advantage."

They could not counter these claims with anything, but were yet too prejudiced to agree with them. That is the power of the idea which, once having set root, takes from us the ability to hear rational reasons and to judge impartially. The doctor sensed this bias and said, "We will not speak further about this here until letters have arrived." — Frohbart suggested that then they would have to wait a long time. But the doctor remained of the view that it could not be long, the authorities would have to step in if they did not want to put themselves and the land in danger. Thus eight days passed where they hung around in society and in the area without making any plans. On the ninth day the doctor went, as usual, to the post himself in order to see whether letters had arrived for him. This time he received one from his sister who gave him quite clear information about the affairs of the fatherland and its intrigues. He hurried to the hotel to inform his friends of it and read out to them the following letter.

Dear brother! — I do not indeed know whether this letter will yet find you in Metz; only, I am convinced that you, in the case that you should have travelled further, will have made arrangements to receive it anyway. In the short time of your absence important things have taken place. In our district everything is in uproar and nothing is spoken of but rebellion which would have had to have broken out in a few days if the authorities had not succeeded in tracking down the intrigues and arresting the ringleaders. Amongst these are people from all classes, clergy, artists, professors, lawyers, foremen, merchants, writers, and who knows how many others. All these have been arrested. The detained indeed went without a racket, with the greatest possible considerations, you could say, with politeness; only the prisons in which they are being kept let it be concluded that it must be very serious. Büttmann, the financier's son, is also amongst them; his mother, who is attached to him with extraordinary love and whose happiness and pride he was, finds herself since his imprisonment in an unconscious state and they despair of whether she will every recover. Steinwart's Gustav and the lawyer Frohbart have also been asked about, but have gone away on business, and the parents were given the instructions to call them back. The sons, I think, will surely this time be so clever and not obey their parents. I spoke to Gustav's mother. She is indeed sad, but yet more composed than I expected. She seems to know her son is in safety and does not grieve anymore over his absence, of which you do not know how long it could last.

Dear brother! You will hopefully with your constant travelling here and there not have allowed yourself to get into any such associations where they could get too close to you and we would have to tremble for you. You are certainly too upright for any unlawful undertaking, only it seems the uprightness does not suffice this time for being innocent; because people have been drawn in to whom no stain clings. Just imagine, the chaplain Dörr, who is considered in the entire district to be a model of decency, is also amongst those imprisoned. This could make me worried for you, hence I ask you to write to me soon and tear me from the painful uncertainty. N. N., P. P., and all acquaintances say hello; I give you my sisterly love.

This letter had made a powerful impression on the two young men. Gustav looked like a corpse. Frohbart ground his teeth as if he were in a desperate struggle, although overcome, not yet able to imagine himself vanquished. The doctor, who had expected this mood, said, "Be calm and rejoice in your safety. Of a return to the fatherland there can be no talk anymore for the time being. Thus continue in another world where the people pay homage to other ideas and in the intention of making everything work out; but only because they are themselves of dust, do they stick to dust. America is the land which you must get to know in order to reach the standpoint of seeing humanity in its true and not just in its ideal, chimeric worth. Everywhere there is good, but also everywhere there is the imperfect, and it cannot be any other way because the human himself, from whom everything emanates, is a mixture of good and evil. Only a few individual humans are capable of utilising the good in themselves so that it obtains dominance; if this is the case, how is it to be assumed that all of humanity, or even just one people, will ever rise so high that you will not find slag and defects anymore? Tolerance is the highest virtue of humanity; anyone who possesses it stands on a higher step because he does not devote himself to vain hopes and does not expect of every tree in the forest that it is a giant tree. So much for today. I have letters to write, accounts of my journey to give in order to not in the end fall under suspicion of having been of assistance to you in your flight. Tomorrow, when we will have properly digested the news we have received, we want to make firm plans for the future." Both friends went depressed to their room and felt no desire to go out or be amongst people.

***

Ebb and Flow

The next morning the two friends came very subdued to the doctor. Frohbart especially felt deeply shaken in that he saw the progressive system attacked at the seams and humanity hampered in its growth for centuries. Gustav was of another mind. He thought from the investigations there would emerge what would have to happen in the future; the authorities will come to the conviction and see themselves forced to seek a firm standpoint to produce the nation and to choose for this a head amongst themselves who has the entire fatherland to monitor and its members to lead. The doctor listened to this jeremiad for a long while and finally, after they had exhausted themselves in tirades, expressed his views with powerful conviction.

"My two friends are genuine patriots and thus of a mind that it would be a pity if they were not to become the closest friends because of differences of ways for the fulfillment of their love for the fatherland. Different paths are in life very often struck out on for one and the same goal, without that the freeman is led astray thereby, meanwhile the short-sighted, pedantic man is as a result induced to hate and persecution. The difference of paths divides the power of humanity and hinders it mostly from performing something great. Thus it is also with you — the spirit of party wrecks your undertakings, even if they were expedient, already in advance. If you then consider fully the spite which stands betweens the parties, and seeks to draw advantage from each, then it is no surprise if all the eccentric cosmopolitan plans fail and expose their advocates to scorn. But as soon as we observe rationally and see in the history of all times and nations not only in political, but even in religious respect, always the same phenomena, then we shall finally conclude that nature does not want any violent revolutions, rather it wants to grow, flourish and bear fruits according to specific laws. You will allow me after this preamble to examine your views before you and to console you that none of your ideas have been realised.

A constant progress of culture with any one species is an idea so contrary to nature and reason that it provides us with proof that the human, when he wants to climb higher than nature allows, is thinking of perversities. Everything moves in eternal laws given by the creator. These possess stability; in their effects, however, they are subject to a constant change. If a real progress were able to take place, it would have to happen through changed laws; but since this is not the case, cannot be the case, all changes which we see or intend are not advances, but rather only changed effects of unalterable laws. Free will is a characteristic which every human possesses. One uses it to obtain fame, the other to obtain wealth. Here one tames every urge for time-consuming pleasures and undertakes a difficult work which often takes up his entire life; another goes at the double through life and conquers from every moment as much as it can give him.

Is with all these cases surely a progress to be seen? No. It is the power of will which you raise to a degree agreeing with our nature, but cannot increase. Can you surely think of a world where the rivers, instead of into a sea, always flow onwards? Where would they come to an end? In the deepest depths where no falling and rising and nor progress is possible anymore. Do you find amongst the plants or amongst the species of animals even a trace of growth of a species? It is so infinitely difficult that any one being achieves its highest perfection determined by nature that we extremely rarely find it both with plants and with animals. If it is now considered so difficult to develop entirely there, how much more must it be the case with the human where the delicateness of the body already demands so much care that he seldom becomes that which he could have become or should have become. If we now consider fully the spiritual development, oh, how many accidents is it not at the mercy of. Here one comes and preaches reason, there another and says exercise the feelings. — Here one teaches religion, there another politics. Here one praises diligence, there another genius which leads without effort to the goal. Of an inner natural self-knowing no mention occurs at all anymore, because you assume the human must have stood in his primitive state far below the animals and must have learnt from them. Is all this, I ask once more, surely progress, or is it the natural doings of every single individual in the species? — Indeed the genuine propagandists say that that is all correct; but humanity languishes in darkness and must be led to the light. To the light, I ask. What is the light which the human lacks and can be given? — 'Enlightenment' is the answer. — Well! Over what should you enlighten them? Over politics, national budgets, over law-giving, constitutions and their continual improvement? Eh, look though! In the end you want to yet make a jurist out of the countryman? — Here I say: if you ruin a countryman, want to make from a contented citizen a discontented one, I would like to maintain, into an unhappy human, then you fill his head with political ideas and he will, instead of tending the field for himself and his family, go into the tavern and with dreamers waste not only his time, but also his means.

To the extent humanity is destined for an uninterrupted progress, it cannot count on any political fortune, thus it has nothing else to enjoy but to constantly hope and fear and never rejoice in a perfect maturity. And in which conflicts do you not then have to enter with the institutions of state, with the civic laws, with community ordinances, even with family customs and with your own conscience? If humanity shall constantly grow, then it is a duty to promote this growth under all circumstances and with all powers, without consideration for means and ways and to get the opposing obstacles out of the way, and then nothing can then come but reformations, revolutions, and destruction of all that which does not agree with progress, without consideration for whether it is in the moment holy and beneficial to humans. It is thus an eternal war which becomes conditionally necessary through the propaganda, whose advocates plant their victory trophies on overturned thrones, on wrecked items, on burnt out places and scaffolds."

Gustav interrupted the doctor, since he was pausing, and said, "Good doctor, I hear from your words the views of my friend Brandheim. Oh! If he had to atone for his probity, his diligence, his love of the fatherland with prison and ignominy, then the world would deliver proof that it is incapable of valuing virtue and prefers to build on pillars of slavish minds and of baseness, than on magnanimity. But, I hope the judges themselves will see the truth of his views and instead of punishing him, will pull him out of the darkness in order to help bring about the state which must be the most beneficial for not only the people, but also the authorities. The world has been set in motion like a wheel rolling down the mountain and no salvation is to be hoped for until you put a stick in its spokes, bring it to a standstill, and thereby save the lands from the downfall."

Here Frohbart wanted to interrupt the speaker; but the doctor hindered him from doing so, in that he said, "Propaganda and conservatism are the two opposites of which neither is suited to human society. They are the poles of humanity at which no love and no happiness either germinates or blooms. In the moderate zones fruitfulness, warmth of life, and cheerfulness reign. Thus away from the poles! Let us transfer ourselves to an unforced emotional life where we do not always have to be afraid of either running into the progressives or the men of conservatism. But, you will ask, if neither progress, nor conservatism can be suitable as laws, where then is the road on which you can wander safely? — The answer is that eternal growth is a chimera ... An unalterable stability is contrary to the laws of nature and its powers. Humanity does not grow, but it changes according to the circumstances of the time, though not in its essence, rather in its use of the means for satisfying its destiny. But from this it also emerges at the same time that standing still or stability is just as much contrary to nature. A lake which has no outlet and no inflow would begin to ferment, thicken and turn into a poisonous morass. The sea itself must accept rivers into itself, drive the water in subterranean channels through the earth, form wells, springs, rivers, and streams, and thus accept again into itself what was given out. Here there is neither growth nor stability, but rather an eternal circulation, a constant ebb and flow which keeps everything in activity and preserves it from degeneracy. In this activity a seeming progress is certainly preserved, because nowhere reigns rest, nowhere standing still; but it is nothing more than the necessary circulation of blood of the life of humanity. Breathing in and out, pushing out from itself and drawing into itself; striding forwards and backwards, these are activities of creation which rest on irrefutable laws and bring punishment to anyone who stands as a hindrance in their way. Everything comes from the origin and goes again to the origin. In this movement we see nature in its whole like in its parts, with winter and summer, with spring and autumn, with plants and animals, with being born and dying; in short with all the movements of the universe. We must pay attention to such laws, draw from these the norm for our ethics and politics, then we will see that the humans are not so bad at it as hypochondriac preachers of conservatism and restless propagandists want to whitewash us as. You will certainly ask: what is the origin of humanity? What is the ebb and flow of its life? How is the progress and regression in it so difficult to unite in the way we see with rivers and sea, with ebb and flow, with return of the seasons and finally with the circulation of blood. A look at the spiritual nature of the human will enlighten us over this. Listen!

 The human is of twofold spiritual and sensory nature. Over the activity of the senses nobody is in uncertainty — for nobody will want to claim the first human loved his wife in another way, and the meals, even if only fruit and herbs, consumed with smaller appetite than occurs in our time. The senses of the first human were just as sharp, perhaps even sharper than our own. Over this we are clear. But now we think to count and measure the spiritual characteristics, as are there, the feeling of independence, the skilfulness; the reckoning of the day and the night, the dividing of the seasons, in short everything for which power of thought and comparison with other things occurs was not inborn, but rather taught and was better comprehended from century to century. There is no talk that education is a certain teacher, but the means of understanding the lessons, applying them to oneself, lies in the nature of the human, and hence he would, if he received no experience from without, make himself such as to still his urge for knowledge. It is not the outer phenomena which enrich the human; but the ability to take into yourself such things, to compare them and to make them your private property, is a gift of primal law which asserts itself under all circumstances of life. The diversity of education made no difference here. The builder cannot speak so delicately as the scholar, also cannot make any logical conclusions, by contrast the learned professor cannot guide any plough, cannot sow and reap, and cannot lead any rural household. If here a fundamental examination could be made, then it would turn out that you encounter far more maturity of life amongst the country people, as amongst the townspeople, and that they do not have to regret that Hegel and Kant have not yet strayed into the country schools. Considered from this point of view, it will not seem to us so paradoxical anymore to consider the first humans to be just as perfect as those now. We thus see the human on his earthly course supplied with everything and equipped with powers which can lead him through life and can make it pleasant for him. Only there is in him yet another means, or better, another urge which seeks in a supernatural realm satisfaction and this is the urge for self-preservation for eternity. The human gazes into himself, becomes aware there of a light which he can entertain at will; hears in himself a voice which instructs him over the circumstances of the here and now to the hereafter and feels in this way bound to eternity, to a life judge and strives to unite with him and makes himself into a creature for earth as for heaven.

Here is the point at which the human can learn to recognise the duties towards himself and others. He is destined for two worlds and now asks himself whether the duties are the same for both of them, or whether we have to sacrifice more for the one than the other. To the extent we consider the matter uninhibitedly, the duties are the same in that only those who bring to the here and now the proper tribute, also provide for the hereafter; and those for whom the hereafter is dear, the here and now must be thankful for their existence. Without the here and now we would not have become, just as we are not capable without the prospect of the hereafter of appreciating the here and now. We have accordingly twofold obligations, for the here and now and the hereafter. For the here and now in that we utilise understanding, reason, and experience to rule it according to circumstances and to always seek new sources of satisfaction of needs. Here an apparent progress enters, apparently, I say, in that it does not place the human species in its essence any higher, but rather directed only according to the circumstances changed through the prevailing conditions. In the beginning most institutions had a more or less spiritual tendency; but since in the hands of humans everything is sensualised, you are always required and will always be required to create new institutions in order to tie the spiritual bond ever again anew to God, to morals, and to higher human dignity. Everything ages, everything becomes outdated, and there the old must then always be refreshed again or be replaced by something new. What rational man can surely call this progress or rather growth? That would be exactly as if the farmer, after he has ploughed the field, wanted to say he has obtained a new and better field; of if he, since his field had become as such unusable for him through flooding, had it lie as a meadow, but in exchange transformed a meadow into a field, wanted to say he had become richer through this new arrangement. The human had also in spiritual respect already from his origin on everything and if he had not withdrawn his spiritual characteristics into the sensory world, then here a conservatism would have been expedient. But since this was not the case, will never be the case, the human is thus called to an uninterrupted activity in order to take care of the realm of the spirit and to replace again the losses suffered. We have accordingly two realms, time and eternity. Time urges ever forwards, eternity stands eternally still. The human urges forwards when he serves time, he goes backwards when he gazes at God. The human, drawn through sensoriality, distances himself from the origin, but must necessarily return again to it if he shall not become a victim of time. This is then the ebb and flow of life, that you daily serve the world or the senses, and also daily see the origin.

I well know that such views are not suited to our times. Dispositions which are filled entirely with politics cannot have any idea how there could yet be something which stands above their doings, or even equalled them. They think that with the upswing of material interests the soul itself soars just as certainly, where not yet more certainly into the realm of the spirits, as if they were giving fitting sacrifice to their spiritual life and looking around for its laws. But it remains inexorably true that the more stubbornly the politicians adheres to his ideas, the more his heart is closed to eternity and he becomes in the end fanatical over his perverse views in such a way as only the most bigoted bigwig can be for his superstitions. Ebb and flow, breathing in and out, the alternation of day and night, rise and fall of the stars of the heavens, the human's spiritual and moral culture, everything stands under one and the same law. Everything pushes from the origin out into the world of the senses in order to then come back individualised to the origin. The circulation of the blood in humans and animals is the truest image of this activity. Forcibly, even with blows, the blood goes from the heart and returns in calm, ordered gait to the heart. Our activity must direct itself according to such primal laws, then we are world citizens, are patriots and can thoroughly assess what needs be done for humanity and what the right means are to be of use to it. When one attempts it, and goes early in the morning, before he begins his worldly day's work, with his thoughts and feelings back into his inner home, to God who reveals himself to everybody who seeks him in earnest; he does the same after the business of the day, before he goes to bed, and he will find how ripe his understanding becomes, how calm his feelings, and thanks the eternal one that he placed a law in us which cannot be denied if you do not estrange yourself from nature and strive to connect time and eternity appropriately. This, I say it once more, must be the basic principles of a true patriot and friend of humanity who wants to see humanity placed not just on a chimeric, industrial or political height, but rather on the standpoint of his natural, temporal and eternal destiny, where no vicissitudes can rob him of his new possession and destroy the peace of his heart."

The two friends had listened to this lecture with the greatest attentiveness and seemed for the greatest part, especially Frohbart, to agree with it. But Gustav suggested that in this way humanity would also obtain no stability for eternity because it would have to by necessity stride from one doctrine to another, from one institution to another. The doctor responded, "Contemplate carefully what I have said, and you will find that stability is taken care of just as well as movement."

***

Self-Reflection

When the two friends had left the doctor, they felt in a mood for which it would have been difficult for them to account. They also for the first day did not speak about what they had heard and abandoned themselves, apart from individual reflections over humanity and its position, to their own contemplations and went, without visiting the barroom, to bed after a simple supper. The next day, when they had dressed and taken in breakfast, Frohbart, who was not made for brooding to himself for a long time, finally broke the silence and said, "We find ourselves in a situation which makes it difficult for us to look into the future with an impartial disposition. The fatherland is shut off from us, even if not forever, nonetheless for many years. We must thus obtain the courage to learn to consider ourselves to be strangers in this world and to obtain a view for life which makes it possible for us to endure it bravely. We entered into a labyrinth without keeping a secure exit open for ourselves, for that we must now atone and can do nothing about it but undertake this atonement with manly strength. The doctor held up a mirror before us in which we could see ourselves clearly and obtain the conviction that we too, if all our plans had succeeded, would have seen ourselves driven onto a sandbank on which in no case would roses have bloomed for us. His ideas of spirit and sensoriality, of ebb and flow, of time and eternity, have gone to my heart in such a way that I see for the first time how dangerous it is to get mixed up in plans for the improvement of the people and the world, before you have yourself become mature."

Gustav, sitting at a table, his head leant on his left hand, had listened to these words without moving. He sat upright and replied, "I was raised by pious, religious parents who made every effort to teach me in this respect the same dispositions. For a long time I kept the religious mind; but since I surrendered myself to political ideas, since the belief imposed itself on me that acting for the fatherland was the highest religion, the feeling for a divine religion has entirely died in me, and I see myself pushed out into a realm of material interests where no goal and no boundary is to be seen. Oh, had my parents never let me out into the world, had they made me into a farmer who through the simplicity of his business remains tied to nature and God, it would have been better for me than being in possession of my attainments which, considered exactly, are nothing more than fruits of refined sensoriality, which exercises all the more force over us than they possess spiritual touch and entice us through mendacious shimmers into the abyss. Friend, I do not know whether I will ever find myself again, or will succumb in the struggle which stands before me."

Frohbart, no less ardent for truth than Gustav, no less moved to see his goal missed, saw with open eyes into his life. He possessed the peculiarity of having to speak about all the phenomena and feelings of life; through that he placed fortune and misfortune as objects before himself and analysed them for as long as until he either obtained clarity or at least satisfaction. He said, "Friend, we have been cheated, and indeed not perhaps of a piece of gold, no, of our temporal happiness. The doctor ties to the temporal life also an eternal one, it is thus about whether we want to also be cheated of the latter. Ebb and flow, he says, is the image of human life. I believe he is right. We previously thought otherwise; you desired a constant ebb and I a constant flow. But it did not occur to either of us that for an ebb or flow a sea is required, and hence we worked away as if we ourselves were oceans and ebb and flow must emanate from us. We were fools; and it is good for us if we see that; then we suffered a shipwreck on an island full of pearls which can replace many times over the loss which the shipwreck drew from us."

Gustav sighed from the depths of his soul. "Were I alone," he said, "I would endure it, would find means of spending my existence and where possible of coming to a new life of the soul. But my parents, my mother, they will survive my absence, but not my shame."

Frohbart replied, "They will endure what is not to be changed, and if they have such a disposition as you say, then this must console them and led them strength to bear the unchangeable with religious composure." Gustav responded, "The solace of religion must be powerful for such who possess religion; but when the religion itself offers a new cause for grief, if my parents consider me lost not only in a worldly respect, but also spiritually, even in a religious respect, then must not their pain be much greater, even unconquerable?"

"You are tormenting me", Frohbart said, "with self-made sufferings. Your parents will learn that you live; the doctor will inform them over your disposition and then they will certainly compose themselves."

Here a silence occurred. Frohbart began to smoke a cigar. Gustav drummed the fingers of his right hand on the table. Finally Frohbart stood still, placed the cigar on the table and said, "The doctor is a clever man. He has divided the life before us into two halves, of which the one belongs to time and the other to eternity. Had we formerly had such a division pointed out to us, we would not now be finding ourselves in this sad position. But what are we given in this respect? Nothing, almost less than nothing. The Christian religious principle in which we have grown up has been pulled so far out into the world of the senses by philosophers and theologians that a reversal is hardly to be thought of anymore. The old orthodox forms to which a part of Christianity still adheres are for young people, for students, so inexpedient that their observance works still worse than if you do not know them at all. You go to church without knowing why. You hear sermons and teachings which do without all of nature and comprehensibility. The example which we see in others, even in professors, is also not made for drawing us back into a sea of eternity. The head is filled, but the disposition is left empty and there nothing remains but to finally connect with ideas of reorganisation which have the best for humanity, which you think to be deliberately oppressed, as the intent. Now we stand here, robbed of all prospect and do not know to what we should fix the marrow of our life, the love for life. To become a pious hypocrite is one thing to which I could not decide to do under any circumstances; — without such a step, however, I do not see how it could be possible to satisfy the views of the doctor which convert a spiritual ebb and flow into a necessary condition."

Gustav had risen from the table, was looking out through the panes of the window without wanting to see anything special and said, as he turned towards Frohbart, "I stick with that if would have been better for me to become a farmer, where I would have retained the natural, child-like beliefs in God. As student, as scholar you can not believe anymore because that which you should believe is either not shown at all or in a way that it is completely opposed to the nature of other academic subjects and the character of university life, and you declare an academic believer already in advance to be a talentless and feebleminded idiot. In this way the religious feeling is suppressed and the animal nature obtains dominance under blazing forms of scholarship, in that we think then that we live for the intellect, whilst we only rehash what others filled with the spirit have taught. Error reigns amongst humans — they seek a goal without knowing whether it is the right one, and when they finally see themselves betrayed, then they accuse the fate which did not want to fit in with their one-sided ideas. I would like curse myself; would rather not live in order to not have the torment of being ashamed of myself."

He fell silent. A deep silence occurred. Silence is for the displeased heart the most unbearable, hence Frohbart began to sing:

> It cannot always remain so
> Here under the changing moon, etc.*

---

* [Tr.: "Es kann ja nicht immer so bleiben" by August von Kotzbue (1802), music by Friedrich Heinrich Himmel.]

Self-Reflection

After he had sung a refrain, Gustav said, "I am going to the doctor. He is a man who has the look of having fate in his hands. He must know a life principle which stands above the university philosophy and the deceptive ideals of cosmopolitanism and a screwed up patriotism. He shall offer me a staff from the treasure of his experiences on which I can continue with new confidence along the road of life. I will ask him with bare words whether to work for humanity is not the only service of God. And to the extent he denies this, he shall tell me in what way the ebb and flow desired by him is to be produced."

Frohbart agreed with him and said, "Yes, we will go to him. He has helped us out of one labyrinth, but led us into another. Someone who can say A must also be able to say B. He shall give us a light for our pilgrim's path so that we do not plunge into new abysses."

***

The Passport

They went to the doctor and met him counting out bills of exchange and currency for his two fugitives in order to send them further as soon as possible, and to travel home himself again in order to divert from himself any suspicion of aiding in their flight. At the arrival of his friends he closed his writing desk and said, "I have made the effort this morning to sort out your passes and to get hold of travel money for you. I must not linger abroad any longer, even for you the stay here is not healthy, hence we must part. Fate stands commanding over us; we want to obey it in a manly way, by that we blunt all its thorns and can keep ourselves connected, since everywhere the same sun shines, with its rays. If you follow my advice, then you will travel from here, without lingering anywhere, to America where other men, other customs will offer you new life views which, even if not compensating for what is lost, can though enrich you with new experiences."

Gustav answered, imbued with emotion, this address with, "Good doctor! Friend of my parents and of us, what we feel for you could not be expressed with words. You are the true, the practical philanthropist, for you offer your hand to those who need help, and do something essential, whilst we strive to convert, even if not the entire world sea, a part of it into fresh water. What gave you the insight and the power to escape the enticing images of a general influence and to offer your hand only to individuals who are needy of such? Teach us this secret so that the shimmering phantoms vanish and we, as we ourselves only have special individuality, will guide our effectiveness also only to our nearest environment."

The doctor offered him his hand and said, "What I can give shall be granted to you. It is little; if you understand how to use it, however, it is a lot and for you and others profitable. — Humans are in the delusion of only achieving something essential, beneficial through influencing others, and do not suspect that through this eternal leadership, through this constant guardianship you deprive the human of his highest jewel, of his freedom. The human must mature himself, build his own life road, then he will stroll in a happy mood and becomes conscious of his own power. An imposed welfare is no welfare, because it did not come from a free source. The self-obtained possession is worth gold, and even if it were to contain nothing but lead. The human considers himself, induced by humans themselves to do so, to be a natural guardian of others, or to be a natural beggar. From this relationship, from this false idea arise all the disparities and unpleasant circumstances of human life. The animals in the forest are free, the human thinks he must command or beg. Nobody stands on their own two feet anymore, everybody worries and takes pains over others; the others, however, let themselves be taken care of and reproach the provider if they do not exercise the usurped guardianship properly. The guardians think they are doing a lot of good, meanwhile they are only serving their vanity. The one imposed upon believes through gestures of thankfulness and humility that they can bribe heaven, meanwhile he surrenders himself to idleness. Thus the world stands before us and is not to be changed until a primal state occurs again where the human is ashamed to impose or to be imposed upon. Give the hungry wanderer a coin for his further travels, for the rest nature, if he remains true to it, will provide. Oh, how much is to be said over this. The evil of the world does not lie in the forms of government, nor in the institutions of state, but rather in all the humans at the same time, because they have either made themselves into slaves of arrogance or into slaves of humility."

Both those present had listened with great attentiveness and when the doctor fell silent, Frohbart took up the conversation and said, "Good doctor, you have me gaze into a mirror where life appears to me in a wondrous, but yet clear light. The human is a bad, foolish creature who always criticises, whereas he himself is full of bad habits and weaknesses. You are right: the human must be able to be free, but not according to the way of the cosmopolitans who would like to bring everyone under one norm, but rather in his usual, independent action and inaction. The human is of such an odd nature that an imposed good does not once have real value for him. Irregardless of that we always want to lead, teach, and lecture and do not think of how difficult it falls on us ourselves to be always trained and controlled. I will from today on impose a view on nobody anymore, will not talk anyone anymore into drinking, so long as he has no thirst, but will also not bend before any world improvers and philanthropists, but rather ask them who gave them the right to relieve others of their duty of self-action. Thank you, good doctor! The idea of this general beggarliness, where the rich beg with beggars and the beggars with the rich, has let me see at once human life so clearly that I may almost believe myself capable of not straying anymore in future."

Gustav could not pull himself together so easily. The idea of how difficult it is to achieve the goal of life occupied him too much for him to be able to content himself with a free individuality, like Frohbart. "I am connected to humanity with indissoluble bonds, through father and mother. Nature has taken me under its guardianship, which I cannot extract myself from without becoming a criminal. My life belongs to my parents, wherever I may linger. To repay them through training in that which human nature encloses in itself of the beautiful and good is my goal, my indispensable goal. But here I lack the means and the ways. You have, good doctor, have allowed us to take a look into eternity. How can you lift the veil entirely? Are there no other paths than those through the church of orthodoxy and dogmatism? What can America offer me for this end goal? Will I be required there to seek out specific districts of my confession of belief or perhaps go amongst the Quakers? Do not let my questions irritate you into not listening to me. I must air my heart so that I also give you solid motives for the solace of my parents. I ask you, how can you arrive at eternity? How can you connect with God? Is working for humans then not the purest service to God?"

Gustav looked at the doctor full of expectation after these questions. The latter said, "We do not need to arrive at eternity, we are already in it. The elements of nature, the visible as well as the invisible, are all from eternity and remain in eternity. Everything which exists is comprised of primal elements. That which is put together dissolves, but not an atom perishes. Life is of the primal elements, therefore cannot perish. It is only about connecting the animal ego with the positive inner life's ego so that both become one, then we are with our ego in eternity. The idea is as simple as if through combining several ingredients you prepared a tasteful meal where you did not recognise at all the coarser character of them anymore. To learn to seek out the inner ego, to think and even discuss and speak with it is a purely human and philosophical task which actually anyone who only to some extent lays a claim on the ability to think should develop. That person would thereby do something essential for humanity in that he places himself in the position to give testimony to a life principle without whose knowledge and compliance you wander constantly in darkness.

To connect with God is after the solving of the above task a need of nature. The fulfillment of that law, however, is subject to so many scruples and opinions that you often barely know how to help yourself. Church and the obligation to attend church is contrary to our nature without you be able to give an account of why. — Go to America where the religious principle is treated in an entirely different way to how it is with us, and therefore fear missing your goal anew. In America there are, as in the entire world, many different religions. The rational person should ask themselves once more with this variety whether there is not also a primal religion. As soon as this question must be answered with yes, the following question: 'Whether surely the religion has arisen from the religions, or whether this has arisen from that', will be answered of itself. The sea did not arise through the rivers, but rather the rivers arose through the sea. The multifarious lights of colours have not produced the sun, but the sun produced the colours. Everywhere the individual emerges from the general, from a large whole. Thus with religion. An eternal life's sun exists which reflects in the inner-being of the human and leads him without special guidance to the goal. The Bible itself gives the clearest intimations over it. First under Enos, the son of Seth, you begin to preach the name of the lord. Previously you knew him without sermons. First through Moses was an imperative, positive religion introduced. What those first people possessed and knew cannot remain closed off from us if we have the courage to seek the primal thing in us and separate it from the imposed and accidental. Therefore go confidently to America and put up your cabins there where the sun shines in the most charming way and contented people will come towards you. But seek there the teacher and preacher Enos in yourself so that you learn to speak and comprehend the name of God.

The question of whether working for humanity is not the true service to God is answered by the unprejudiced man of itself; for the orthodox man, be he rationalist or pietist, a sufficient explanation is easily given because he seeks everything abstractly or meritoriously and believes no reward is worthy without such. It is almost not possible for the human to believe in an innate, positive worth. He always thinks he must bear on himself somewhere an external sign of service in order to be able to be regarded as human. Not what we are, but rather what the world says of us is the judgement which we think we are required to subject ourselves to blindly. The oak greatest worth consists in that it is an oak, the greater worth of the human is to be human.

According to what has been said it is to be asked what the principal peculiarity of the human is. — The human can recognise themselves, he thereby raises himself above all other creatures. The human is created for self-knowledge, and his entire striving from youth through to the grave is directed to it. Certainly he entered for the achievement of these goals various paths which did not lead all to the hoped for goal. But the urge to know themselves lies in all, from the lowest to the highest. What urge shows itself already in the youth to be the most violent of all? — Certainly the urge to distinguish yourself. Everyone wants to be looked at and admired, in this urge all are the same. But in their ways of looking at themselves, humans distinguish themselves from one another. One party strives and works outwardly in order to see themselves in their works; another party seeks the worth of the human in the inner-being, in themselves, and believes thereby it is getting closer to the solution.

The first way of looking at oneself is the the great Babylonian empire which has no boundaries, where each believes he understands it the best. The farmer sees himself in his fields, the war hero in the battle, for the orator conciseness of talk serves as a mirror, for the poet the meter of the verse. The curser takes pleasure in brutality, the pious in the timidity of gestures and in the drawn out tones of his speech. The clergyman places his image between heaven and earth and cannot see himself satisfied in this glorious position in that he thinks himself to hold in the one hand the key to blessedness and the other the judgement of the judge of the world. — In none of these branches is positive self-knowledge possible, however, as little as you can use the image in the mirror for handicraft.

We see in life a form of looking outwards which is not to be praised enough on account of its usefulness and its services, but which can the most easily seduce and be seduced directly because of its holy appearance. This is the supporters of the poor and suffering of all classes of humanity. There is no more beautiful virtue than to feed the hungry, clothe the needy, support the sick, and console prisoners. Only as soon as the virtues are put on show by the banner of vanity, then they are also the most seductive, because their lustre blinds us and hinder us from seeing the blemishes which attach to our inner-being. Have the left not know what the right is giving is a commandment, comprehended from the nature of the human, but which is rarely properly understood and valued.

From this is also explained to what extent the having an effect on humans is true service to God. Have the left not know what the right gives is a doctrine which finds use everywhere. If the demagogues had won, would they surely have taken to heart this saying and not have let the left know what the right had done? — I hardly believe so. To the contrary they would have written their deeds not only on parchment, but on iron and stone in order to be able to reflect themselves in it for the future. Enough, up to here no true service to God takes place. It is a moving out into the sensoriality whose rule is all the mightier, the more religious the tendencies are for whose sake you proceed. It is difficult to not let the left know what the right gives, and hence we do not find satisfaction on any of the above paths and must seek to look at ourselves from another side in order to arrive at a certain goal of self-knowledge.

The human has innate, inner characteristics, an innate positive worth. The images externally which he sees in self-made mirrors are hallucinations, even less than shadows. In the inner-being, however, are those powers which make the human into a human and give him undeniable independence. Now it is to be asked what are the principles of the human which distinguish him from all other creatures in essence. — The most distinguishing power of the human is speech. Through this he constantly raises himself to new knowledge required by the times and to free will. — But where does speech arise from? Where is its root? Is it in the mouth or in the heart, in the head or in the limbs? — Here you torment yourself for an answer and do not realise that nature has given it already long ago in the most unambiguous way. The language of the human lies in his figure, because if he did not have this he would not be able to speak. But the human, you say here, does not only speak, he also thinks! — Entirely right; he thinks, but with what? Answer: he thinks by means of language. Were he not able to describe the features of a matter with names and words, all thinking would stop. Thinking rests thus also on the capability to speak. The human can speak externally and internally. Speaking externally is the usual way of making yourself understood in important and unimportant circumstances of life. Speaking internally, or rather speaking in the inner-being, is thinking. Only this inner speaking is also again subject to its own temptations and difficulties. There are free and sensory thoughts. If cleverness gives the brain-teaser and digests it in the inner-being, sensoriality penetrates as far as the innermost sanctum of life and plucks wickedly from the tree of divine knowledge. But when we give the inner speech, the inner thoughts complete freedom, then it obtains infallibility and teaches us as the word of God what we are to do and let happen and what the true service to God is."

Here the doctor fell silent. His two friends did not interrupt the silence with a single syllable, so that he saw himself induced to continue speaking and to say, "You do not seem to be satisfied yet, only I know of nothing more to unveil right now. May it also appear little in your eyes, it can though serve as a seed from which for each of you your own tree of knowledge can grow which gives you imperishable fruits of truth. I will add to what has been said the following indispensable moral rules. — Preserve the love of humanity in yourselves, it is the first commandment. Keep pride in your human dignity so that you never sink into baseness. Never do anything over which you would need to be ashamed before your parents, friends, or other virtuous people, then you will both return again to the fatherland and rejoice in it with unfeigned devotion."

The doctor now told the two friends to go to their rooms in order to pack and arrange everything so that they could spend the evening amongst each other undisturbed. They did that. The day passed with preparations and the evening amidst thousandfold instructions for home. The doctor had made the arrangement that his fugitives would travel from Metz in their own carriage. In the morning, after everyone had already taken breakfast, the carriage arrived, the luggage was loaded up, and the doctor said, "Now farewell! Do not forget me, however it might turn out. Take these writings, they contain the basic ideas of that which I have been speaking about with you these past few days; they are the talisman which will keep our souls connected, even if lands and seas separate us." He wanted to part, in order to avert a further saying goodbye, but Gustav held him back forcibly and said, sobbing loudly, "Console my mother. — We want to go. Whining is of no use except to make you soft." Gustav let the doctor go and called out, facing east to his home, "Mother, forgive me. — Oh, mother, to not curse me! Forgive me!" — He sat down as if he wanted to recover. People came into the room. Frohbart seized him by the arm and led him with the help of the doctor to the carriage. The postillion, who perhaps had already seen

The Passport

such scenes, remained in his seat and flew along the road and out the gates with his two travellers.

***

America

The further travel experiences of the two friends offered little of interest. They arrived in North America in a land which had often served for them as an ideal, only was far behind their expectations. Frohbart, the progressive who had constantly spoken against the German aristocracy, found there a financial aristocracy which seemed unbearable to him. Money was the flywheel of the civilisation, of the good note, of the culture, was the central point of all rights and duties in civic as well as domestic life. Beautiful arts and positive sciences were so little respected as if they were tolerated strangers which you obtain for money, but can also lack with money. The uneducated and raw pride of a rich American woman seemed to him to be a degeneration of the natural dignity of the woman and he once said to Gustav, when he came home from a large party, "To the first baroness whom I encounter in the fatherland, if I ever return home again, with the noble natural manners, with the self-consciousness of their superiority, not only through birth and wealth, but rather through certainty of speech and of behaviour, I will kiss their hand and take care in future not to place all under the law of a humbling equality where also no trace of an elevated culture is to be seen. It is not the reading of social writings; not the imitated nobleness which only produces affectation, but rather the rhythm learnt from youth on, the freedom of movement, the courtesy without losing face, the certainty of giving attention now to only one person and straight afterwards to the entire company; these are things which must be exercised from youth on in order to obtain that pose, as if nature had itself given them in order to show a concept of genuine feminine dignity." With Gustav natural good-naturedness kept the upper hand, he responded to that utterance with, "Nature has only one true aristocracy and this lies in the awakened disposition of the women. The upper classes lose themselves mostly in conditioning; and be their behaviour ever so beautiful, it remains without informality though cold and stiff. When I by contrast consider my mother, how rich and poor female neighbours turn to her in all affairs, how even the noble woman in tangled up cases herself seeks advice and help from her, then I say, he who has found heart is the true noble, the others warm themselves in his light and are happy in when things occur to find assistance with a man of integrity. In this way our exiles observed life and prepared themselves thereby to be able to judge character which was to be of unpredictable use for them in later years.

Both had to much sense of honour to let themselves be supported by their families. It was also not advisable to remain in open correspondence with the fatherland because they could have given cause through such for court summons, which they would have to either obey, or through disobedience stimulate the authorities of the fatherland still more. For this reason they did not indicate their place of residence to their parents either and satisfied themselves with news which they learned from immigrants.

They had through their knowledge already established a secure subsistence and thereby came into contact with all the classes of inhabitants of the rich city of Ph. Gustav could write as if it were engraved. He drew excellently and understood the laws of geometry fundamentally. With these three branches of learning he obtained an income with which he could have easily nourished a family. In order to not be required to go from house to house, he provided instruction in all three subjects in his residence, and formed a sort of school. The German professor became well-known in a short time and it lay only on him to give the greatest possible expansion to his institute. Frohbart played the piano very well and sang as well. This made him, connected with a pleasant talkativeness and the diverse knowledge, which was related to family and state circumstances, into a beloved member of all society great and small. He had found in America what many sought in vain, a free and secure income and would have been able to feel happy if he could have put himself in harmony with the character of the Americans. But here everything stood contrary to his expectations. He had believed in finding in the land of a young freedom nothing but progress and propaganda, and met a conservatism against which the boldest ideals of Gustav seemed to still be childish dreams. The entire land had been forged to an indestructible money bloc and to the throne of a material goddess of freedom which made it incapable of any movement forwards or backwards. He expressed himself in this respect to Gustav, "The Americans have achieved the zenith of conservatism. What they are now, they will remain and preserve from rotting only through striving for wealth." Gustav was able to find his feet more easily. The steadiness of the state institutions did not displease him and if the yearning for home had not filled his heart so much, he would have been able to decide to spend his life in America; but it went for him like Ulysses, who only wanted to see the smoke rising from the chimney of his parent's house once more in order to them die with joy. Only this was not begrudged him so soon, and hence he endeavoured to recall in his memory the teachings of Doctor Braun and to devote himself to the study of a deeper knowledge of human character. He still recalled his teachings well enough to draw constantly from himself with such researches; but that became so difficult for him that he often despaired at succeeding. His surroundings, but mainly the yearning for the fatherland which was becoming all the stronger, the more he withdrew himself from external objects, hindered him constantly to gaze calmly into himself and arrive on the trail of the roots of his urges and powers of knowledge. When he spoke with Frohbart about this inability, it was revealed that the latter, even if with changed views, still had the demagogy stuck in all his limbs, and he would never have arrived at the goal if chance or a kind fate had not given him a new guide.

*****

A New Star

One afternoon Gustav took a walk. When he wanted to return to the city again, a rain shower descended on him and forced him to seek shelter under the verandah of a summerhouse. There he met another walker who had fled there with the same intention. They greeted each other, spoke about the changeability of the weather and about the whim of fate which led them under one roof. The stranger asked whether it was an accident.

Gustav did not cotton on straightaway to the sense of this question and said, "Everything which was not previously destined or arranged is accident." — "Would it not then be possible", the stranger asked once more, "that a destiny had led us together here?" Gustav expressed how he could not imagine such a grounds for fate. "It comes down to then", the stranger continued, "whether one of us might not be called upon to be of use to the other." Gustav could still not come to terms with such a question and suggested that in such a case you would then have to consider the use to be the fruit of a happy accident. The stranger replied, "We do not want to argue over words whose interpretation is only too often subject to accident and should hold ourselves to realities. To this end I will allow myself the question: where are you from?"

Gustav: "From Feg. in Germany."

Stranger: "And are seeking here?"

Gustav: "I sought safety and found it; but now I seek contentment."

Stranger: "And hope to find it here?"

Gustav: "I do not know. It seems it does not reside on the other side or this side of the ocean."
Stranger: "Then your seeking is probably in vain?"
Gustav: "I fear so."
Stranger: "With truth resides contentment."
Gustav: "But where is truth?"
Stranger: "Poetry says:

> Only in the heart gleams the mirror of truth,
> Only in the inner-being do we find it easy
> That the spirit with unaltered seal
> Offers us the crown of certainty."

Gustav: "Does not the crown hurt?"
Stranger: "Like the sun when it shines too bright."
Gustav: "We are then accordingly damned to an eternal twilight?"
Stranger: "No; you can get used to the sun."
Gustav: "I have not yet known anyone who could gaze with rigid eyes into the sun."
Stranger: "That is also not necessary if we only see clearly the objects which it illuminates."
Gustav: "But then we never learn to know ourselves!"
Stranger: "Is it then not enough that we stand in the light and are illuminated and warmed by its rays? Is it necessary that the laboratory assistant tests the heat of the fire with his hand? — He knows that fire gives heat and begins the work with confidence."
Gustav: "In this way we subject spiritual activity to a natural mechanism."
Stranger: "Should that not perhaps be so? Would an unnatural mechanism be better? Here is the deception which humans constantly play against themselves: they want to be supernaturally spiritual in order to be permitted to be all the more naturally sensory or material."
Gustav: "That I do not understand."
Stranger: "The human seeks the spirit outside himself, indeed, if it were possible for him, outside of creation and does not think that the further he distances it from himself, the less he learns to know it."

Gustav: "That is probably true, and hence we must hold ourselves to given laws."

Stranger: "Quite right. But we must also learn to test these laws for whether they agree with the spirit."

Gustav: "That is not necessary if we believe."

Stranger: "I believe in the honesty and punctuality of my bookkeeper, and nevertheless I look through the accounts which he draws up for me."

Gustav: "That is distrust."

Stranger: "It is the exercise of the most beautiful gift which the creator has given us, whereby we obtain self-conviction."

Gustav: "Is such necessary?"

Stranger: "As necessary as your own palate in order to be able to taste food and enjoy it with appetite."

Gustav: "Who will subject the laws of God to a critique?"

Stranger: "Wanting to recognise a law does not mean criticising it. Nobody can fulfil a law which he does not know. Hence God gave us the power of thought in order to test what comes from him and what from humans."

Gustav: "Only the human can reveal himself to the human."

Stranger: "Then we have no divine law."

Gustav: "Here is the rock face on which I and many thousands who sigh after truth fail. We are supposed to believe, and what? We are supposed to believe in miracles because God cannot reveal himself to us without miracles. Hence I said just before that examination is not necessary if we believe."

Stranger: "But if we do not believe anymore, what then?"

Gustav: "Then examination should be possible."

Stranger: "And you consider such a thing to be entirely impossible?"

Gustav: "Sometimes, yes. But then there are again moments where all of nature, where my own nature seems to call out to me: investigate and examine."

Stranger: "Well and then?"

Gustav: "Then I strain my understanding and reason in order to obtain light for myself, but the further I think to penetrate, the darker becomes the path and I return sadly to my first standpoint."

Stranger: "In order to urge forwards anew!"
Gustav: "In order to doubt my powers anew."
Stranger: "Courage alone leads to the goal."
Gustav: "From where shall the courage come, so long as I am in uncertainty over the matter?"
Stranger: "The matter is not to be doubted, humans merely waver in error over the means of achieving it."
Gustav: "Let spiritual powers investigate?"
Stranger: "Yes."
Gustav: "With what means?"
Stranger: "With understanding and reason. But there we must not consider understanding and reason to be the spirit itself, but rather only outflows or tools of it."
Gustav: "If understanding and reason are not the spirit itself, then we have no spirit."
Stranger: "That is exactly like if you said: when the brush is not the painter himself, there is no painter at all."
Gustav: "Accordingly understanding and reason would be merely organs of the spirit?"
Stranger: "No less."
Gustav: "What, however, does the spirit actually consist of?"
Stranger: "It consists of feelings, loves and hates. It resides in the disposition of the human and gives to it a specific character. Its entire being is word, is speech. It has built the human for speaking, so that the human by means of speech can penetrate into it and connect with it. The letters are its elements, the words are descriptions of its ideas and concepts, from which understanding and reason arise."
Gustav: "But how is the spirit to be recognised?"
Stranger: "Through looking within yourself, hearing and feeling. But anyone who wanted merely to look would never obtain the vibration and the elasticity of life which are essentially needed for thinking. He would never feel joy and love, never feel raised to a higher existence. He would look out into the eternal ether and lose himself in the blue of the sky or in the countless stars. Anyone who merely wanted to hear would not see the blue and the starry heavens. All colours, forms, and beauties of nature would be lost to him and he would have no positive means of preserving his

individuality independently. What would happen to the one who merely wanted to feel? Such a one would have to dissolve sunk in delights and pains and forgo independence. Seeing, hearing, and feeling are the powers of life which once connected create the entry to the sanctum of life. But certainly this seeing, hearing, and feeling must not only be directed outwardly, but rather inwardly, towards the deepest lying organs, even to the marrow of the bones, then we are approaching the powers of life and may ask them for light and truth and protection. — Only the rain has stopped, we can each follow our road; but beforehand ask once more whether surely only chance brought us together."

Gustav answered quickly, "No, no accident, rather a kindly fate has led me to you, and I ask you to consider this important discussion to be the beginning of a new friendship which must for me be of the most fruitful consequences, and to allow me to be permitted to visit you." The stranger wrote his name and residence with a pencil on a card, and handed it to Gustav with the assurance that he would be delighted to be permitted to look forward to his imminent and frequent visits.

***

The Development Periods

When Gustav arrived home, he told his friend about the acquaintanceship he had made. He rejoiced over it and said that to him such an opportunity was extremely welcome and he would take part in the visits. Gustav replied that he wanted to make the stranger aware of it beforehand, who on account of his openness would be pleased by a double visit. On the third day Gustav sought out his new acquaintance and found him just as amiable and courteous as he had been under the verandah of the aforementioned summerhouse. He spoke with him about many things and revealed to him the wish of his friend Frohbart to be permitted to share the visits with him. The stranger declared that with him anybody was welcome who desired instruction over his life views. "But in order to know whom you are confiding in," he continued, "I want to tell you though who I am and what fate led me to America. My name is Bandorf, I am German, am the son of a not unknown chemist who achieved important things in that subject. I dedicated myself to the sciences, and since I did not want much to subject myself to the forms of a rigid civil service, I chose for future career the teaching profession. I received in respect to my diligence and gifts undivided praise, but then an evil fate decided that a book dealer would publish a small work by me in which the teaching profession of that time was drawn with sharp strokes and was taken by the chancellor of the university to be referring to himself. The latter had important friends at court and amongst the civil servants. The book indeed was not banned, only I was called to account and received the intimation that with such beliefs I must not count so easily on a position. Because it had never come into my mind to insult anyone personally, and my protestations were not heeded at all, I was outraged over such a process and renounced the life course I had taken up. At the same time, now fifteen years ago, my brother died here in America and made me his heir. In the feeling of affronted honour I left my fatherland, moved here, and used my time for the study of a higher philosophy, to which humans did not venture to critique and at most declared the lover of it to be an eccentric. What I have obtained this way exceeds the bounds of all sciences so much that I have come to the sad conviction that the entire world wanders in darkness and has lost the laws of life, in a word paradise, right down to the last trace."

Gustav responded to this, "Paradise is lost, traces of it you see in Asia. But to the extent paradise is a law of life, I well see that you will not find there what you seek. Show me the entrance to paradise so that I will learn to pluck from the tree of life."

Bandorf replied, "The entrance to paradise is hard to find, not because it is too far, but because it lies too close. You cannot believe that God could have pressed together all his sublime characteristics in such a narrow space as the human takes up. Even if you finally see this truth, you end up erring anew because you want to place it in the head or in the heart. The scholar thinks and says, 'In the head is paradise.' The romantic feels and does not let anyone deny to him that God could only reside in the heart. The old master builders built cathedrals and temples and thereby produced an image of paradise, that is of the human. Those great artists, however, put not only one altar, but several altars in their temple; on every pillar, on the walls, even in the backmost parts and in the side alcoves stood such and gave the proof that they did not limit the knowledge and veneration of God to a specific part of the body, but wanted that extended to all the external and internal organs of it. The first doctrine which you can therefore provide to someone seeking truth is that of getting to know themselves at all the altars of their life and their body."

This view was for Gustav as new as it was though clear to him immediately. "The human", Bandorf said, "possesses many varied talents; it is therefore necessary that each of them has a special root of origin. If it were merely the head in which the life of the human enclosed itself with all its spiritual powers, then the wolf with a human head, or even with a wolf's head which had all the organs of the human, could think just as well as the first philosopher. But since this is not the case, since no human head grows on a wolf's body, no wolf's head though can possesses reason, we must necessarily consider the entire body to be a temple and all the inner organs, namely the stomach, kidneys, bladder, liver, lungs, heart, etc., to be altars within it where we place our sacrifices so that they rise up as sweet scents to God." Gustav, surprised by the novelty of these ideas, said, as Bandorf paused here, "You astonish me with what you have said, only it must be true because chance could not have built such churches. Thank you for sharing this enriching view and I will strive to get to know the altars in me as much as possible. But in order to attain this goal sooner, I would like to ask you surely to describe for me a sort of process. Everything which nature wants to give us, you should indeed seek yourself, only the experienced man has formed a theory, knows small means or advantages for obtaining this or that, and you, since you speak with such certainty about the matter, have certainly already long since drafted a plan according to which one arrives safely at the goal." —

Bandorf replied, "There are admittedly means and advantages which make the progress much easier, only they are of the sort that most investigators step back in surprise at their simplicity, in that they consider the means not only to be insufficient, but also to be childish. But in the assumption that you, in the case you also put no belief in the process, will not attempt to make a joke of it, listen and take note for the time being of the following.

The mouth is the reproductive organ of the inner, spiritual life. The mouth, as the material tool of speech, must be able to send back words and letters into the ground from which the lips, tongue, and palate grew, then the entire body is raised inwardly and outwardly to speech, to the power of thought; our ego which we speak inwardly into obtains the ability to place itself in all parts of the body, at any altar it likes, in order to express and lay down its wishes there. This is for the uninhibited the entire doctrine, in that it agrees in the most exact way with everything which we do in the world. To the self-conscious person years of explanations and entire libraries give no information. Anyone who has the courage to consider the speech elements spoken in the mouth and also syllables and words to be a sort of bodily meal, and even to swallow them down in the same way, will soon sense what glorious nourishment he has taken in and how necessary it is to nourish the spiritual life not only with dull concepts, but with elementary powers."

Gustav had listened to this short method of procedure with astonishment and replied, "How can the human speak into himself, since he perceives no sound there?" Bandorf responded, "But he can feel inner sound or resonance. Externally, in the air, bright, loud sounds are required for our physical ear; internally the sound is lost to the external ear; on the other hand the spirit hears and feels the word thought in the mouth and becomes in contrast to the pronounced word, ever stiller, ever more powerful."

Gustav shook his head at this last explanation, but not from doubt, rather from astonishment at not having long since hit upon such a simple doctrine himself. He said, "I believe I have understood you. In order to raise a beautiful flower, we must place the seed or bulb in appropriate soil. To grow flowers in flowers or from flowers is against nature. Indeed, even the thriving of plants does not depend directly on the tending of them themselves, but rather mainly on the soil from which they come, and we thinking creatures neglect the fields, the temple, the altars, let them rot uncleaned, and do not suspect that we prepare though this heterodoxy itself the downfall. We turn and twist our feelings for so long until they finally harmonise with the forms of the school, storm to the high altar and call out from there to the crowds, 'Look, it is I who read this and that book and have attained conviction. In the regions of the spirit the human has become so much a child that he thinks the sabre makes the soldier, the brush the painter, and boasts with knowledge which, far distant from being our property, can be forgotten at any moment. I will endeavour to arrive in the temple and to learn to feel the speech in me, but rely in this activity on your support so that I do not stray from the correct path and waste my time on detours."

They spoke still more about what had been said for further comprehension, and when Gustav thought he had comprehended everything properly, he left Bandorf with feelings of the most sincere thanks.

***

Stability of the Laws

On one of the following visits Frohbart joined Gustav in order to also get to know the American sage face to face. America corresponded to his philosophy of progress just as little as he could not yet give up the idea of eternal growth of the human race. He often said to Gustav, "If humanity cannot grow eternally in its culture, even does not have to grow thus, then it has never grown, and the first human was as perfect as the thousand-millionth member of his descendants. But since this is not possible and contends against all experience, I declare in America, as I did in Europe, the propaganda is the true priesthood of humanity and only when one day everyone has gathered in its temple will the world enjoy the happiness which was destined for its inhabitants from the very beginning."

Gustav had already long since liberated himself from all ideas of world improvement and sought, but without success, to divert his friend from such cosmopolitan ideas which were never to be realised. But Frohbart stuck to his views and planned to speak with Bandorf on this subject. Hardly did the opportunity present itself, when he was visiting him with Gustav, to make a few remarks about this subject than he did so, and Bandorf responded, "You want to have humanity grow all the way to infinity. Now I ask, on which law could such a growth rest. Everything which humans do is exhausted in its nature, in its law, the new thing appears to us always only in the changed practice of the laws known since the very beginning." Frohbart seemed not to have entirely grasped the sense of what had been said, hence he replied, "Just from the altered practice do new laws again arise and so on for all eternity."

Bandorf: "Can humanity learn to count in a different way to when it happened in the very beginning?"

Frohbart: "According to the form, yes."

Bandorf: "No new law arises through the form."

Frohbart: "I think it can."

Bandorf: "You can count particular things, sum up and subtract from one another. A new way is not thinkable and goes against all the laws of reason."

Frohbart: "But in what diversity do counting and subtracting occur?"

Bandorf: "That changes nothing. The law remains, and without a new law you cannot raise humanity any higher."

Frohbart: "You are condemning out of hand the most glorious characteristic of the human race, in that you are enclosing it in dead laws and with it abolishing all freedom."

Bandorf: "Directly through the solidity of the laws and through the constantly new use of them the human becomes free. Were he not capable of exhausting the law, of grasping it entirely, he would hover in eternal uncertainty. If on the other hand the same constancy were to lie in the exercise of them, we would have no change, no joy, no prospect of a gladdening hereafter. We are in the position to grasp the laws of life and to rejoice in this certainty; but we exercise them under ever new forms and attributes, hence the stimulus of life and the desire to preserve it for eternity."

Frohbart: "What you are saying surprises me, but I think I have understood you. The art of counting is in its nature exhausted, but in practice infinite. The laws of harmony are perfect in themselves in such a way that you could promise the rule of the world to someone who was in the position to set a new turn to them. Geometry consists of three lines with which we calculate all surfaces, magnitudes, distances, and even the course of the stars. I concede entirely to you that in this nothing more is to be done. But should not there be new laws still to be found? Would it not be possible through a rational progress to arrive on the trail of constantly new laws and thus lead humanity every closer to its perfection?"

Stability of the Laws

Bandorf: "When you hope to find new, i.e. not yet discovered at all, laws of nature, you are right to teach progress. But in the case such a thing is not possible, then you are building on a hope which is never to be satisfied. It is thus to be asked whether we lack some law. Are our needs not all to be satisfied by the known laws? We want to see that. The first need of the human is to communicate, thus speech. — This communication should have conciseness, logic. — He wants to reside with his family not only comfortably, but also corresponding to his feelings of order and beauty, the art of building. — For the expedient building, in order to satisfy all ideas, much must be performed which you cannot perform with mere hands, mechanics. — The human does not only want to speak, but rather express his feelings yet numerically and even melodically, music. — The human measures heights and depths, measures paths and steps, and divides everything which belongs to him and others into specific magnitudes, geometry. — We see the stars, want to measure the heavens and put them in agreement with the earth, astronomy. — Over these subjects we are clear in such a way that to their nature nothing can be added anymore. Now it is to be asked, what does the human desire apart from these? What wishes still stir in his inner-being which he could not satisfy through the laws described above? — Two fields lie before him where he does not see clearly, whose laws you either have not yet found or seem to have lost, and these are: laws of a best state institution and — laws of our final destiny, of immortality.

Over the laws of a perfect state institution, humans write and speak a lot, but can, when it is suitable to go to work practically, never arrive at the desired goal, because for utter specialities you lose sight of the generality in which alone a positive law were to be found. A generality, however, is not to be found as long as you are worried about local circumstances, about nationality and temporal events. The art of counting to five, of drawing with straight and bent lines, of singing the scale of seven notes, does not belong especially to any time or any people, because these laws are contained in every human. We see in all law books traces of such a generality, but which lies so hidden that only the practised eye sees it. But no state institution can be perfect as long as the human does not know his uppermost destiny, and does not know for what he is called to life. Here then arises the question, does the human achieve his highest destiny as a member of the state? Or should the state institutions be considered to be means of achieving that all the more certainly? If the first takes place, then religion and philosophy are superfluous because then physical force would have more effect than all the principles of morals and virtue. But if the second case occurs, where the human destiny is above the circumstances of the state, then this becomes serving or mediating and gives only such laws which promote the highest goal, and distances everything which endangers it. The idea of a perfect position is accordingly a problem until the religious principle is ordered so that it becomes as clear to us as the multiplication tables are to the calculator and the colours to the painter."

Frohbart had followed this lecture with all the sharpness of his intellectual powers and said, when Bandorf fell silent, "I am happy to have finally found a wise man who has the courage to bring state institutions into harmony with the destiny of the human. But directly from your basic ideas there emerges the necessity of a progress, in that we can achieve the primal lawfulness and an ennoblement of human nature only through the perfecting of state institutions. The human only learns through mistakes and only then, when the authorities will have learnt to see that their institutions do not bear the desired fruits, will they feel forced to seek the general, the primal lawfulness, in order to secure their own existence and that of their subjects. In that the propaganda remains, even if a worrying one, a necessary evil though."

Gustav wanted to interrupt his friend here. Bandorf, however, hindered him from doing so, in that he said, "Allow my just a few words as a reply to the propaganda."

He continued, "Propaganda, you say, is an evil, but a necessary one. Propaganda is war, is an incessant revolution. War and revolution destroy what seemingly stand in their way. I do not want to ask what those who perish in the struggle gain for it, but rather ask, what do they those who have escaped the destruction gain? — Impoverished, wrecked cities, depopulated lands, displeasure and despondency on all faces, hardship, hunger, and plague are the usual consequences of violent shocks to the state. Can such a state be suitable for making humans attentive to a higher destiny, for thinking of an ennobling, and for erecting institutions for that? Certainly not. Theft, murder, and mugging are urges which awaken with dejected circumstances in the heart of the human and they lead to the return to a wild state instead of to ennoblement. And you want to prepare such a state for our glorious German fatherland which gleams above all peoples of the earth in moral, religious, social, and legal respects. That would be directly as if on a great table which is divided into many fields, where everything were more or less contaminated except for one single thing, you wanted to also smear this in order to produce a sort of equality. Germany must not ever be revolutionised. It stands as a model for all the lands of earth. Even if not politically great, it has spiritual stability, sees itself supported in all districts, has no colossus for a capital* which swallows everything. Everywhere there is truth, emulation, culture, art, and learning institutions. Though here and there pettiness and crooked views may also prevail, they have no influence on the whole because no state can deviate too far from the norm of the others. Germany approaches the ideal of a best state institution so much that only the addiction to fashion and the Gallomania peculiar to the Germans is capable of failing to appreciate it. When in Germany the spiritual-religious principle, as much as it reigns in the people, is also properly comprehended and followed by the clergy and officials, then the paradise is reproduced not in Asia, no, in Germany, and from all the heavenly directions emissaries will come, not in order to teach, but rather to learn and to spread what has been learnt into all regions."

Gustav, to whom this argument seemed quite natural, felt forced to express his views and began, "Our enlightened patron has through his discussion portrayed the state of our fatherland so rightly that I barely comprehend how in youth one can be taken in so stubbornly for either conservatism or progress. Both are necessary, both grounded in nature, but

---

* [Tr.: note that this was written before German unification, when Berlin was only one of many German state capitals.]

lead, if you only pay homage to one, to a one-sidedness which embitters the heart and leads to a fanaticism as if those of a different mind were not members of the great family of humanity anymore. Here, my friend," he continued, turning to Frohbart, "is the point which I previously sought in vain, which must unite the adherents of propaganda and of conservatism in the most intimate way and bring human society again into gladdening universality. Previously there was a division between us in this respect, which indeed had no influence anymore on our hearts, but often brought us into small conflicts which only our tolerance made into a principle was capable of setting aside. The dividing wall is now removed and we want to recall this moment always with joy, when a blind prejudice fell from our eyes and we could be true and honest friends even in the field of politics."

Frohbart offered Gustav his hand and said, "You are right. Previously there was still a divide between us. It has fused together and connected both parts into one. I feel as if newly born and can barely comprehend how it was possible to remain so long in blindness." All three were after these declarations extremely pleased and parted with the resolve to assemble once every week in this way and discuss the most important affairs of life.

***

The Best State Institution

When they had assembled one evening, they again came to speak about the laws of states and their occasional change. Their previous ideas still clung to the two friends so that Gustav considered any alteration of law to be an attack on the rights of the people. Frohbart on the other hand saw in an expedient change and reformation the happiness of the peoples. Bandorf had been listening for a long time and finally said, "What you, my friends, are claiming is on both sides true. You should take care not to lay your hands on natural laws, i.e. on such as agree with the most necessary needs of humanity and its social order and are as it were conditioned by it. On the other hand there are accidental laws which are tied to events and institutions, which in arise in time and achieve their goal in it. Who would like to have a law persist when its aim has been achieved? Here the human must prove the worth of his aim and his wisdom. Here he must show that he stands above the mechanism and knows how to seize the moment of life spiritually and how to assimilate. Anyone who wanted to reform without necessity would, instead of improving, destroy; anyone who on the other hand did not have the courage to pursue the spirit of the times a little would be a pedant and would, instead of benefiting humanity, harm it. The human has understanding and reason, he feels and knows what is fitting for the time. If he sets to work free and uninhibited, if he opens his heart to the love of humanity, then everyone to whom it is the responsibility to do something seizes the right thing in order to keep on course the necessary events. Considered from this viewpoint, the duty also grows for us to develop the spirit, to study history, to get to know all the institutions of wisdom in order to draw from them wisdom for us and others. Anyone who proceeds in this way will preserve themselves from any one-sidedness and be in a position to perform for humanity that which the circumstances demand."

Frohbart contemplated what had been said for a few seconds and said, "In this way progress and conservatism are necessary conditions of the state and general life. But who teaches here recognising the law, and who, when it is recognised, gives the power of exercising it?" Bandorf replied, "The knowledge of the destiny of the individual as well as of the whole."

Frohbart: "What is the destiny of the individual?"

Bandorf: "That he meshes with the whole, but at the same time frees his spiritual nature from any pressure."

Frohbart: "Can he do that as long as he is bound to the whole?"

Bandorf: "He can so long as no hindrance is present which obstructs him from thinking and feeling."

Frohbart: "Religion places shackles on us."

Bandorf: "Beneficial ones."

Frohbart: "How can shackles be beneficial?"

Bandorf: "When they hinder us from harming others."

Frohbart: "But if I am not of the same mind as others?"

Bandorf: "Then I keep my own for me and leave the rest for them."

Frohbart: "But where I am required to join in their ways?"

Bandorf: "To the extent the necessity is there, you do it."

Frohbart: "Against my conviction?"

Bandorf: "It remains your duty to mesh with the whole, but at the same time to preserve your own, spiritual freedom."

Frohbart: "Can I join in customs which have no value in my eyes?"

Bandorf: "If the whole commands you must. Nothing is more dangerous than offence. If I steal from my neighbour a fake coin which he considers to be genuine gold, then I have committed a theft of genuine gold. If I take the sacred appearance from customs which he considers to be holy and drag them down to indifference, then I have sinned against the law of brotherly love in that I have stolen his heaven from him."

Frohbart: "Accordingly I would be obliged under given circumstances to participate in ceremonies which could stand in complete opposition to my views?"

Bandorf: "Absolutely. Do we act any different in everyday life? Do we not fall into line in order to not annoy according to the characteristics of our teachers and friends? Parents and educators are guided by the peculiarities and talents of their children and students in order to not impact them. Why should we then for the love of our weak neighbours not respect their long venerated customs?"

Frohbart: "You are right. We live not only for ourselves, but mainly for the whole, and there it would admittedly be a great presumption to want to desire that everyone else direct themselves according to us. Only what can we do for others under such circumstances?"

Bandorf: "That is the most harmful pride of the human, that he always thinks he must have an effect on others, teach and train them, meanwhile though nature has given everyone everything to come to maturity. If it continues as it does in our days, then we will arrive in the end at the idea that the human is not in the position to eat and to drink properly if he has not learnt it through history. We live in a time of the most shameful ignorance and if I may ever reproach my fatherland, the glorious Germany, then it would be over that the leading elements of it have let themselves be seduced by the view that the germ of religion and of all spiritual institutions lies in history, and it needs only a few historical documents to arrive at the wisdom of Solomon and all the perfection of human nature. The human needs nothing but himself in order to recognise himself and arrive at wisdom through his self-knowledge. If everyone then knows themselves, the happiness of humanity is produced and conservatives and propagandists must leave, and the historiographers must see their foolish striving and connect to the whole whether they like it or not."

Frohbart: "But then the human has no means anymore for doing anything for others, for obtaining distinction and commendation!" —

Bandorf: "It is true, in such mentioned state the individual human would certainly not have so much foolish work as now. But instead his activity would be approximately that of a healthy tree in the orchard which protects its smaller neighbour from storms. Each tree must sprout its peculiar fruit itself and no other tree can be of assistance to it in its growth."

Frohbart saw the truth of what he had heard, he obtained the conviction that the great art of developing humans consists in the end in letting their powers work undisturbed and at most bringing their attention to them. He said, "How often our revered friend Braun in Germany spoke in this sense; but I was too superficial, or rather too stubborn, to understand such simple truths. Fate had to take me to school in order for me to finally learn to hear and comprehend. I will seek to digest what you have shared with me so paternally in order to finally become, even if no wiser, yet a not completely ignorant human."

Bandorf rejoiced over these convictions. Gustav also joined in and said, "My friend Frohbart has a heart of pure gold. He would give his blood for the happiness of others. But he is too impatient, and wants to force humans to be happy. But humans, of this I am completely convinced, do not tolerate any force in spiritual respects and would feel happier with self-selected evil than with imposed happiness. I walked the opposite path and wanted to force humans to see in order to thereby capture the happiness in their circle. Both paths are individually of no use. In the alternation of moving and standstill the true life of the individual develops as does that of the whole, and hence I will dispense with all hypotheses for the future and seek the truth free of all dogma both in respect to the state and to religion, and show humans not through vain explanations, but rather through deeds, that we can always ourselves obtain true happiness in ourselves."

Much more was spoken in this vein and the small company parted with the blessed feeling of having come closer to the truth and therefore having fulfilled the primary duty of their existence.

***

Ebb and Flow

When our two friends were with Bandorf one evening, the talk again came to Doctor Braun and his life views. Bandorf was given a report over his position in bourgeois life, over his activities and his doctrines, to the extent the two friends knew of them. When Frohbart touched upon the image of ebb and flow, from which Braun inferred the same activity in all creation and its parts, Bandorf seized on this idea and said, "Such a simile cannot be given by flesh and blood, could not be given by schooling and scholarship, such all-encompassing images can only be provided by the spirit, by the eternal wisdom. Ebb and flow as the pulse of the earth, however, give us the doctrine, how everything, from the grass tick to the highest power of creation, streams to and fro, shows itself in the smallest like in the greatest and also repeats itself with the circulation of the blood in the human body; it gives us a look into the boundlessness of God and nature, where we must marvel at the simplicity of the law and the diversity of the phenomena which arise from it. It is a eternal give and take, an eternal advance and retreat, an uninterrupted pushing out and going into itself again. The law is, as already said above, eternal, the phenomena infinite. When we apply this to the institutions of state, we have the safe norm for a best government. From the head of state, whatever name it has, the pulse must emanate and everything which emanates from it must return again ordered and calm. The government must be energetic from the inside out, then it can rely on everything coming back to it again. A government which must from without push and drive through pashas and despotic officials shows that the body of state is sick, and the blood does not find itself in a regular circulation. To quickly meet such irregularities, where they are made noticeable, to heal the sickness and put the feverish pulse back in order is then the task of the government. Where this art is understood and practised skilfully, there is the best form of government. But since this takes the greatest wisdom, we also only seldom see the task solved and always only by individuals. Now I ask you, where lies the means of always obtaining such regents who understand this high art?

The ideal of a best government has already been realised in republics and monarchies, you thus cannot say that this or that form of government is the better one. But what you can say is that where humanity combines itself with energy, the happiness of a people must necessarily be produced. Now it is to be asked, however, where is a pure humanity? From what laws does it arise? Here we must abandon again the visibility and pass into the realm of the spirit and seek there the root of pure humanity. Sensoriality always produces presumption and too violent a striving externally. The spirit itself finds contentment in itself and desires nothing but that you act in its sense. It also moves outwardly, but in order to nourish and enrich itself spiritually. It likes to see itself in the happiness and the love of others, and where it reigns there is nothing but happiness and contentment. It is thus the spiritual principle which is called to produce the best form of government. 'But how can this principle arrive at rulership?', you will reasonably ask. If right many, stand they high or low, seek the spirit and strive through example to spread it amongst the others for so long as until it penetrates an entire people and thereby produces a purity of circulation that no sickness can infect the body of the state anymore. We thus see here again the necessity for a solid religious foundation fitting to the spirit of the people, from which alone the ideal of a best form of government can arise. Be the government yet so wise and the people have no religious sense, then it cannot perform anything. But when the people are penetrated by pure religious feelings, the government cannot do anything but set itself in agreement with it and perform the most difficult things with simple effort."

Gustav joined in the discussion and said, "If anything is in a position to heal us radically from all demagogy, then it is this discussion. What foolish plans were made in the day and indeed with the best intention, without considering that they, even if they were realised, could not be of any use. You want to spread enlightenment, to make the people aware of perceived or true weaknesses of the government so that they would assert their rights, and did not suspect that the struggle for external rights leads to hate and brutality. If this can be the case with educated and learned men, all the more worse must the effect of such a struggle be on a countryman who does not have spiritual strength enough to be lord of his feelings."

Bandorf continued this talk and said, "Every struggle for sensory, material freedom awakens passions and leads to brutality. Spiritual, inner, religious freedom, however, makes the human civilised and humane. If the enlightenment of the people were to begin in this direction, then all rights and duties would be recognised and the subjects of the state would make their little contribution to the whole with joy. But what happens in this respect? Nothing. To the contrary, the clergymen themselves drag their affair down to the level of the sensory. They deny the most necessary symbols of religion and thereby mess up the whole edifice. Amidst hundreds of journals there is not one which treats the religious principle in the spirit and in the truth; instead of which a criticalness reigns in them whereby intolerance in nourished and from peaceful citizens rational blasphemers or unbearable sectarians are made. The welfare of the peoples must emanate from the individual, but quietly and on the path of pure love of humanity. Everybody seek to explain to their own family, to their nearest neighbour, if he wants to hear, about his essential destiny, then the light will by and by flow through everyone and lead to the hoped-for bliss. This is then the true, I would like to say, a divine demagogy which is subject to no control and no police. This is a light which does not belong to any special class, any special corporation, but rather to the lower like the higher, to the countryman like the townsman, to the unlearned like the learned, in short, to all of humanity. When you have penetrated into the spirit of this demagogy, then I wish that your fatherland will take you in again and collect the fruits of the purest striving from you."

Gustav felt quite stirred by these last words and said, "I will make myself ready to serve my fatherland in this sense and even if I never see it again, the hope shall strengthen me to the last breath of my life." Frohbart, to whom the spiritual life was not yet so familiar, felt at once forced to seize the resolve not only to speak about the matter, but to enter into the essence of it. He made the request of Bandorf to be allowed to visit him once alone in order to be provided special instruction by him like a student from a teacher. Bandorf agreed to that, but remarked at the same time, "You see on what pillars the principles of your plans for improving the world must have stood, when a head of it does not have so much power to seek his own light within himself and yet was resolved to illuminate the entire world." Frohbart accepted this rejoinder patiently and said, "You are right. We were fools, children who wanted to guide the lightning bolts of Jupiter, whilst they did not have power enough to gaze at Minerva's helmet plume."

Frohbart was from this moment on as though transformed. He sought out his teacher as often as he could, and obtained by and by a skill at penetrating into his inner-being so that he kept pace with Gustav and often thanked heaven that he had led him to America. They had to remain in that land for four more years, then the news came from Dr Braun that they had been granted a recently declared amnesty and had received permission to return to their fatherland. They received this news with joy and immediately informed their teacher about it. Frohbart thanked him with an emotion which you were not accustomed to seeing in him. When Bandorf made a remark over it, he replied, "You have made me into a man. Before I always wanted to push forwards; you have shown me the path to the origin and thereby saved my life."

***

Home

They prepared for the departure and spent the evening before it with Bandorf, where he let them look once more into the deepest shaft of his genuinely divine knowledge. With deep emotion, they parted like sons from a father and summoned him to visit the Germany which he had once praised so highly. He said, "That will turn out as it will; but however it does, I will remember you and rely on my image not being extinguished in your hearts."

The next day they went to the ship. The trip was happy and when they arrived in Europe again, they cheered loudly and and travelled day and night in order to be home soon. They met everything as they had left it. Dr Braun had taken care, comforted, and mediated everywhere. It was mainly thanks to his efforts that his two friends were pardoned so soon. They entered their businesses as lawyers again and acquired through industry, honesty, and ethical behaviour the respect of all those who knew them. Frohbart was married already within a year of his arrival home and felt himself to be as happy as he never could have been without Braun's and Bandorf's teaching. He became the father of two boys and a girl. Of the latter, he often said, "I do not know what I should make of her, but the boys I will raise to be men who learn to recognise why they live." Gustav too married in the third year back and was happy. The two friends often came together with their families and regretted only not having their revered friend and teacher also amongst them. As often as they also asked him in writing to come to Europe, he could not decide on the journey, only they remained in correspondence with him for as long as he lived and received some more teachings by which Dr Braun was also edified.

***

Diversity in Unity

Humanity consists of various sorts, but in one point they are all the same, namely in the wish to live eternally. Even the suicidal person comprises no exception here, he takes his life not in order to not live anymore, but rather to exchange the circumstances of his life for different ones. According to this view humanity has an innate stamp by means of which no individual goes unrecognised, whatever colour he wears and whatever language he speaks.

So much of the whole. With the individual we encounter so many deviations that you should think humanity has divided itself divided amongst itself in order to enliven the whole through diversity. This view is quite right — the unity must find itself in the multiplicity, only then does the whole have a solid worth. How many roses are there? And yet all belong to the same species and comprise a unity. On how many sorts of instruments is music played, and nevertheless there is only one music. In how many sorts of ways do humans speak amongst one another and nevertheless there is in respect to the letters also only one language; thus with all aptitudes and characteristics of humans — they are uncountable, but in the basic urge, in the love for life, not only for the moment, but for eternity, all agree, they want to live and get to know the creator and the creation and constantly receive new impressions of life.

But what emerges for us from these considerations? — It emerges that we should love one another and should hinder any division amongst humans. Just like every instrument meshes with the music and heightens its effect, where none envies the other or wants to have them expelled, humans must live amongst each other, each doing that which life imposes on him and paying tribute in this fulfillment of duty to the whole, each doing what his position demands, there harmony is. But when the second flute wants to rise above the first, there harmony dissolves and the whole suffers under it. Hence it is also the highest duty of each one to do justice to his position with conscientiousness and to fulfil strictly that position to which nature has called him and in which it has placed him. It is not rank and wealth that comprises the worth of the human, but rather the fulfillment of duty, the remaining at the post which nature has allocated to us, where we, without knowing it, mesh with the whole and contribute though to its perfection. Hence everybody always do what your office is, and be this ever so small, you will though receive the full reward.

But here you reply, if that is so, why then do such a diversity of views reign amongst humans? Why can they, gifted with understanding and reason, not decide on unity? Why do they split into opinions and sects where you often cannot find any point of agreement anymore. — This diversity emerges from the many-sided gifts of human nature, where it can appear with the power of creation and say I want to have that in such a way or another; where it is distanced from others and capable of saying this opinion or this sect must not come into my sphere, but that one I want to favour. The realm of the human spirit is too great, you want to close yourself off, become smaller, in order to survey everything all the more clearly. Even this urge lies in our nature; if we use it as a beginning, however, in order to practise by and by considering the great whole, then the suggested isolation is not only useful, but even necessary, so that we remain in a position to preserve the attentiveness to ourselves and to also not lose sight of ourselves in the infinite whole.

If that is so, then you will say Christianity does not fulfil its aim for the whole in that it works one-sidedly and even separates from the others. But directly in that, in this isolation, it makes itself ripe for the whole. It begins its process of development in an isolated society where each can test for themselves where their talents could well be suited;

Diversity in Unity

when he has recognised himself properly in this striving, only then is he capable of stepping amongst humans and guiding them through words and examples, of teaching and showing them their duties. That is just the mistake of so many of our species, that they think only standing in such a post, or having a great sphere of influence comprises the worth of the human. No, in every position in which we stand in life, we can only work for the whole and with it. The basketmaker like the leading official has his sphere of influence, and which fulfils it best of all has the greater worth in that he meshes harmoniously in the whole, but the latter often disturbs the harmony in that he undertakes an activity which he is not a match for. Do what your office is, and do not miss anything there, do with love and joy what it is your responsibility to do, then you will love yourself again and give to yourself and receive from yourself happiness and joy.

The duties of the human are so simple that you must be astonished at why not everybody agrees with one another. But we find ourselves as it were in the hall of a music school where everybody tunes and plays his instrument without consideration for others, and through that a chaos and a confusion arises which cannot be put in harmony anymore; but just listen to this for a little time again and the chaotic fades away and all now work together, even with different instruments, with a unity that must delight our soul.

We are all in the teaching hall. Some tune and play their instrument without consideration for others. When he has the intent of finally joining in with the whole, then good for him, he will feel not only physical, but also spiritual harmonies and set himself in harmony with the spirit of creation.

***

Other works by Johann Baptist Krebs (originally published in German under the pseudonym of J. B. Kerning) translated and published by K A Nitz

Paths to Immortality
Based on the Undeniable Powers
of Human Nature

Christianity
or
God and Nature Only One
Through the Word

The Missionaries
The Path to the Teaching Profession
of Christianity

The Principles of the Bible

The Freemason

Wisdom of the Orient

Key to the Spirit World
or
The Art of Living

And by his student Karl Kolb

*The Rebirth, the inner true life, or
how do humans become blessed?*
In accordance with the words of the sacred scripture
and the laws of thinking

www.ingramcontent.com/pod-product-compliance
Lightning Source LLC
Chambersburg PA
CBHW022015160426
43197CB00007B/449